NORTH COUNTRY QUILTS:

LEGEND AND LIVING TRADITION

Dorothy Osler

Published jointly by
The Bowes Museum and
the Friends of The Bowes Museum

Published jointly by
The Bowes Museum and the Friends of The Bowes Museum
in conjunction with the exhibition

North Country Quilts: Legend and Living Tradition

The Bowes Museum, Barnard Castle, Co. Durham

5 August 2000 – 7 January 2001

(Exhibition funded by Northern Arts, North East Museums and Durham County Council)

First published in 2000

© Dorothy Osler 2000

No part of this publication may be reproduced or transmitted in any form or by any means, electronic or mechanical, including photocopying, recording or any information storage and retrieval system now known or to be invented, without permission in writing from the publisher and the author.

Publication funded by The Friends of The Bowes Museum and Durham County Council

Designed by Blue the design company

Printed by Bailes The Printer

ISBN 0 9508165 2 3

Contents

Acknowledgements	4
Introduction	5
1780–1870 Industrial Revolution and Cottons Galore	7
Focus: Joseph Hedley of Warden, Northumberland	10
1870–1918 A Golden Age and a Sewing Revolution	25
Focus: Allenheads and the Quilt Design Trade	28
Focus: George Gardiner and Elizabeth Sanderson of Allenheads, Northumberland	29
1918–1939 Post-War Changes and New Patronage	47
Focus: The Northern Industries Workrooms	50
1939–1970 Bright Stars in an Age of Decline	61
Focus: Mary Lough and Florence Fletcher of Weardale	63
1970–2000 Revival and the Rise of the Art Quilt	67
Focus: Amy Emms MBE of Sunderland and Weardale	69
Appendix: Quilt Types, Quilting Designs and Quilting Techniques	83
Notes and References	87
Further Reading	88

Acknowledgements

This book and the exhibition which it accompanies would not have been possible without the generosity of all those quilt owners, quilt curators, quilt makers and quilt artists who have allowed their quilts to be included. It is with pleasure that I acknowledge this assistance from: Rosemary Allan of Beamish: North of England Open Air Museum; Deirdre Amsden; Leila Anderson; Maureen Avery; Elspeth Baker-Baker; C. June Barnes; Wendy Baxter; Charles Bray; Emily Brown; Pauline Burbidge; Celia Eddy and Mary Ranby of The Quilters' Guild of the British Isles; Ian Forbes of Killhope Lead Mining Centre, Weardale; Melanie Gardner of Tullie House Museum, Carlisle; Olive Gregson; Lilian Hedley; Beryl Hughes; Helen Joseph of the Shipley Art Gallery, Gateshead (Tyne & Wear Museums); Nancy Lister; Mary and Margaret Pallister; Helen Parrott; Ena Richardson; Monica Sanderson; Claire Scott; Lynn Setterington; Vivienne Telford-Cole; Anne Tuck; Michele Walker; Elsie Walton; and Lena Wright. And, of course, to The Bowes Museum itself whose quilts form the core of the selection.

Financial assistance has come from Durham County Council and the Friends of the Bowes Museum whose generous help has made the publication possible. This is gratefully acknowledged.

Credit for photographs of the quilts goes to: James Austin for figs 104 and 105; Beamish: The North of England Open Air Museum for figs 8, 15, 33, 35, 43, 44, 52, 56, 63, 69, 84 and 87; John Coles for figs 108 and 109; Les Golding of Tyne & Wear Museums for figs 67 and 107; Steve Gorton for figs 102 and 103; Rachel McHaffie for fig 106; and Eddie Ryle-Hodges for figs 14, 37 and 77. All other quilts were photographed by Syd Neville of The Bowes Museum who I thank sincerely for his care in so doing.

I would also like to thank the following institutions and individuals for permission to reproduce photographic and other material: Beamish: North of England Open Air Museum for figs 4, 23, 29, 80, 81 and 92; Durham Federation of Women's Institutes for fig 79; National Federation of Women's Institutes for fig 78; Newcastle City Library for figs 2, 3 and 24; Northumberland Record Office for figs 27 and 28; Edwina Franks for fig 60; Olive Gregson for figs 27 and 28; Judy Hammond for fig 59; and Mary and Margaret Pallister for fig 57.

To the Curator, Elizabeth Conran, and her staff at the Bowes Museum I must extend particular thanks for their logistical help in the stages of preparation – especially Dinah Jones, Aileen Risbey and Rebecca McClemont.

My very special thanks go to two individuals: my husband Adrian whose historian's eye on early drafts of the book proved invaluable in focusing the historical text; and Joanna Hashagen, Costume and Textiles Curator at The Bowes Museum. It is Joanna who has shared the vision of a major exhibition and publication on North Country quilts. The opportunity to have worked so closely together to achieve that vision and show to the world these North Country textile treasures has been a real pleasure. The book and exhibition owe as much to her efforts as to mine – and I thank her sincerely.

Dorothy Osler

Newcastle upon Tyne

INTRODUCTION

The first year of this new, twenty-first century is a timely point at which to reflect on the changes in status and perception of quilts which occurred in the closing decades of the last century, and to view North Country quilts in particular. To carry that reflection further back and chart the full history of quilting in the northern counties of Britain enables discussion of the significance of this regional tradition in time and place. To assemble a selection of fine quilts made in the late twentieth century and set them alongside antique quilts from previous generations provides a graphic demonstration of regeneration, and respect – respect for a regional, gender-specific, vernacular craft which produced some stunningly beautiful, domestic artefacts.

The chance to do all this has been provided through the foresight of the staff at The Bowes Museum, Barnard Castle. With a fine set of North Country quilts in their own collections, a past history of staging quilt exhibitions[1] and curatorial textile expertise, they recognized the opportunity to record, re-evaluate and, indeed, celebrate North Country quilting in the context of the late twentieth century quilt revival. The shift in status and perception of the quilt from domestic artefact to an aesthetic has been significant, both to the perceived value of antique quilts and to the role of the current generation of quilt artists. The impact of that shift on North Country quilting has taken time; just ten years ago it would have been difficult to assemble such a range of high quality, contemporary quilts with direct or indirect links to this regional tradition.

So what precisely is a North Country quilt? In geographical terms, it could be any quilt made in the counties of Northumberland, Durham, Cumberland and Westmorland (now Cumbria), and Yorkshire (Lancashire was not a 'quilting county'). But a bed coverlet of pieced hexagons, though perhaps made in the heart of County Durham, is neither a 'quilt' nor a regionally distinctive one.[2] The term North Country quilting really denotes a style of quilting *per se*, a style with an emphasis on sinuously curving, stitched lines which outline characteristic and diagnostic quilting patterns and lend a subtle, sculptured quality to the quilt. It is the distinctiveness of this style, and the patterns identified with it, which set these quilts apart from other regional traditions of quiltmaking and give a clear identity and sense of place.

The nature of this style and how it evolved over time will be discussed through the chronological sections into which this book is divided. A technical appendix details the structure of quilts, and acts as a glossary for the pattern names and quilt terms referred to in the text. It should be emphasized, though, that this terminology is largely a contemporary one, grafted on to a vernacular regional craft whose original vocabulary was probably limited and now largely unknown. Past generations of quiltmakers might have referred to Patchwork quilts and Strippy quilts, but terms such as Framed and Wholecloth quilts, and setting blocks 'on point', would have been quite foreign to them.

But there is more to these quilts than mere terminology and technical description. They have a strength of purpose, a strong aesthetic quality, and an honesty and integrity which perhaps reflect the social and cultural circumstances in which most were made. North Country quilts were not made in search of social status; they were not pretentious icons of domestic fashion. They were part of a regional culture, a gender-specific way of expressing an association with place in a region which had, and still has, a strong sense of culture and identity. The gender association goes further as some historical accounts show; social quilting provided vital opportunity for women to come together, helping to maintain community and family ties in often remote areas.

Other associations can be 'read' into these quilts. The soft, tactile surface of a quilt can provide comfort, warmth and sensory pleasure and must surely have done so for generations in these northern counties. A quilt may have symbolic or sentimental associations – made as a wedding gift or as a gift between family or friends. The story of the all-white quilt in fig 41 is a touching one. Made by a nanny who stitched one quilt for each child in her care, perhaps it was in part her way of saying, "Remember me". Many of the quilts in these pages are family quilts, passed through the generations with love and affection for the industry they represent and the family members they recall.

One association which can rarely be read into these North Country quilts is poverty. The view that quilts were primarily and originally made by the poor from fabric scraps to provide themselves with warm bedcovers is now discredited. That is not to say that utility quilts were never made nor that scrap fabrics were not used in quiltmaking. But to look closely at these exquisitely crafted, highly decorative, antique quilts is surely to recognize something born of aesthetic pleasure – pleasure in the creating and making of a beautiful, functional, domestic artefact – whether crafted alone or in the company of others. It is a motivation that quilters today will clearly recognize.

Economics did, however, drive the making of some North Country quilts. Miners' widows turned to quilting to generate much-needed family income; women who trained as quilt designers in the North Pennine Dales marked out quilt designs for cash customers; and the two men in this particular 'quilting frame' (Joseph Hedley and George Gardiner) were both commercially involved in quiltmaking. All produced quilts or quilt tops for others to purchase and use.

But whatever interpretations and associations are perceived in a quilt, one vital piece of data that can rarely be read is the name of its maker and the date it was made. Some late eighteenth century and early nineteenth century quilts were signed and dated, but after that it was simply not common practice until the era of the late twentieth century quilt revival. So we must rely on family history, often questionable, or interpretations of fabric and style to attempt to date many of the antique quilts illustrated in these pages. Some, even those in museum collections, may well need to be re-evaluated in terms of age as new research is conducted and new information gained.

The history of North Country quilting is a narrative of culture and community with its origins in that period of such significant change: the Industrial Revolution. To chart that history is to cover the evolution and extension of this regional tradition, then its decline and revival. But the visual reality of that history is contained in the quilts themselves: in the Pieced and Appliquéd cotton quilts of charm and cheerful character; in the soft, sinuously patterned and sensuous Wholecloth quilts; in the bold, unpretentious Strippy quilts; and now in the recent adaptations, even subversions, of North Country style from a new generation of quilt artists.

Map of the old northern counties of England before the early 1970s showing key localities

Notes to the text
Throughout the book, specific quilt types, quilting designs, and quilting patterns with known names (either past or contemporary names) are identified and given initial capitals to these names. In the captions, the old county names of Cumberland and Westmorland have been used for localities in Cumbria, except in the chapter covering the most recent time period when the two counties were combined; quilt sizes are given in metric measurements (width x height) with imperial measurements in brackets to the nearest half-inch.

1780~1870
Industrial Revolution and Cottons Galore

Up to the mid-eighteenth century, quilting had been a professional trade concentrated on London. Quilted items were fashionable and had high status – made for, and sold to, those of wealth and position – but it was not a lucrative trade, as the London Tradesman of 1747 notes:

…quilted petticoats are made mostly by Women, and some Men, who are employed by the Shops but earn little. They quilt likewise Quilts for beds for the upholder. This they make more of than the petticoats, but nothing to get rich by … They rarely take on apprentices, and the Women they employ to help them, earn Three to Four shillings a Week and their Diet.[1]

Despite their low rank and poor pay, these professional quilters were highly skilled and it is in their technical and design skills that the roots of what later came to be the regional quilting styles of Britain can first be detected.[2] Their products were extensively quilted (i.e. stitched through the fabric layers), not pieced or appliquéd, and it is on them that so many of the common patterns later to be associated with vernacular quilting can be found – stylized leaf and flower patterns, feathers, scrolls, the Wineglass pattern and Square Diamonds, amongst others.

Though part of Britain's textiles trade, quilting was not an exclusively professional practice before the Industrial Revolution (fig 1). Quilts and quilted petticoats were increasingly home-made for personal use, as those less affluent began to imitate the ways of wealthier folk by developing and refining their quilting skills to produce 'fashion' garments and domestic furnishings.

Fig 2 Power loom weaving, from Edward Baines *History of the Cotton Manufacture in Great Britain* (1835)

The development of piecing and appliqué skills, which were not so professionally marketable, came from a different source. From the early 1600s onwards, the British East India Company imported Indian painted and printed calicoes and chintzes. Colourful and colourfast, these Indian cottons were much in demand, with precious small lengths and offcuts incorporated into broderie perse and pieced coverlets. So popular were these imports that domestic manufacturers began to imitate Indian textile styles; but these new and exotic fabrics, both of Indian and domestic manufacture, remained expensive and beyond the pocket of most British women.

Fig 1 *A Conversation Piece: Family at Recreation,* Isabelle Pinson, 1781 (French School)
Collection: The Bowes Museum, Barnard Castle, Co. Durham

It was the Industrial Revolution, with its roots in the North of England, that was to bring inexpensive fabrics within the reach of those of more modest means and stimulated the increase in domestic quiltmaking from the late eighteenth century onwards. The invention of spinning machines, patented in 1769, quickly made spinning cotton yarn a factory-based manufacture. This was followed by the invention of the power loom (fig 2) and, by 1820, over 14,000 of these machines were operating in British textile factories, mainly in Lancashire and Scotland, weaving cotton yarn into cotton cloth.[3]

Improvements in manufacturing processes and a fall in wages in the early nineteenth century led to a dramatic reduction in the retail cost of cloth. Edward Baines in his classic book *The History of Cotton Manufacture in Great Britain* (1835) notes that, in 1832, the price of cotton yarn was *one-thirteenth* that of 1786.[4] He goes on:

It is impossible to estimate the advantage to the bulk of the people, from the wonderful cheapness of cotton goods. The wife of the labouring man may buy at a retail shop a neat and good print as low as fourpence [sic] per yard, so that, allowing seven yards for the dress, the whole material shall only cost two shillings and four pence [sic]. Common plain calico may be bought for 2½d. per yard. Elegant cotton prints, for ladies' dresses, sell at from 10d. to 1s 4d. per yard, and printed muslins at from 1s to 4s., ... Thus the humblest classes have now the means of as great neatness, and even gaiety of dress, as the middle and upper classes of the last age ... the peasant's cottage may ... have as handsome furniture for beds, windows, and tables, as the house of a substantial tradesman sixty years ago.[5]

This ready availability of a wide variety of cottons helped channel quiltmaking in two directions in Britain. On the one hand, intricate forms of mosaic patchwork worked by the English 'piecing over papers' method were stitched into coverlets that were rarely quilted. In the early nineteenth century this form of 'quiltmaking' was largely the preserve of upper and middle class women. It was time intensive and needed quantities of paper for templates (not always available in some homes), though it retained a utility form by using fabric scraps. Later in the nineteenth century mosaic patchwork extended to all classes of society. Found in most parts of Britain, it cannot be said to have acquired distinct regional characteristics.

On the other hand, forms of quiltmaking evolved, often in rural areas, which retained quilting as an essential decorative element. These quilts are sometimes referred to as 'country' quilts and, of these, making exquisite 'white-on-white' Wholecloth quilts remained the purest form with fine white cotton used for the quilt top and back. Pieced and Appliquéd quilts of the Framed type, and later Block and Strippy quilts, were made in certain regions of Britain, the northern counties of England amongst them. It was on these 'country' quilt types that regional variations evolved, expressed in particular through variations in quilting patterns – how they were used, what forms of pattern were used and which patterns were combined together.

From the late eighteenth century to the middle of the nineteenth century, Framed quilts were by far the most popular form of 'country' quilt, both in the North of England and in Britain as a whole. Varying in complexity, the variety of fabrics in their pieced or appliqué borders suggest the use of pieces from the scrap bag, though the distinctive chintz panels (figs 10, 11 and others) and some border fabrics may have been specially purchased.

The designs quilted onto these Framed quilts also vary in intricacy. In Cumbria (the old counties of Cumberland and Westmorland) there was a clear preference for using one particular Allover pattern: the Wave. This pattern was almost invariably used on Irish quilts and also appears on Manx quilts[6] suggesting cultural transmission across the Irish Sea. Another marked characteristic of the quilts from these three areas – Cumbria, Ireland and the Isle of Man – is the general absence of any filling or wadding; for this reason, they are considered by some not to be 'true' quilts. To the east, across the Pennines, quilted designs on Framed quilts varied from the simple Clamshell to complex Bordered designs which may or may not be complementary to the pieced or appliquéd design.

But it was on Wholecloth quilts that quilting design really came into its own and it is on these quilts that the regional stock of North Country patterns can be detected more clearly. As in other regions, North Country Wholecloth quilts from the first half of the nineteenth century make extensive use of naturalistic patterns – sprays, baskets and cornucopias of flowers and leaves – all closely worked in intricate style. But they also include border patterns such as Cable Twist and similar chain forms, together with the curvilinear Festoon or Hammock border, and motifs such as Fan, Lovers' Knot, Tulip, Rose, Heart, and the common four-lobed (or Four-petalled Flower) motif whose only known local name is Cuddy's Lug (donkey's ear). All of these became part of the North Country quilting pattern 'library'.

Few in number but fine in quality, the Wholecloth quilts which survive from the first part of the nineteenth century raise the question of who made them. Some are attributed to 'old Joe the Quilter' (see Focus page overleaf and figs 18 and 19), though they differ from each other in style. Another (fig 20) – a particularly fine example – has come out of Allendale and it seems that, even in this early phase of North Country quilting, this dale and its southern neighbours, Weardale and Teesdale, were the paramount quilting localities in northern England.

These dales were also centres for social 'twilting'– families and friends gathering together to combine quiltmaking with other traditional forms of entertainment: music, song and dance.[7] Particularly revealing are the diary entries of Thomas Dixon, a Dukesfield (Northumberland) lead smelter:[8]

1830
27 January   A great twilting at Sparks
2 July   Thunder and rain - Jane twilting
15 July   Jane and Sally at Jacobs twilting -
*   Father and I making a barraw*

1831
9 March   Jane at Slaley [Smiths] twilting

1832
12 April   Jane twilting at our folks
3 December   Jane at Burdus' twilting

1833
14 March   Our folk on twilting in our Parlour
27 March   Jane twilting
11 December   Jane at Nanny Makepeace's twilting

1835
12 February   Our folk twilting in our room

These terse and pithy entries reveal how quilting blended into family and community life – and the pleasure it gave. At the time of these entries, Thomas Dixon and his wife Jane lived to the east of Allendale though Jane came from Allenheads[9] – another hint of the importance of this area for quiltmaking.

Why should these particular dales have developed such a strong quilting tradition? Perhaps because, with a common occupational and economic base in lead-mining, communities were close, a network of interwoven family relationships with shared experience and social activity. And what sort of 'twilts' were Jane Dixon, her family and friends making? Were they making Framed quilts or stitching the beautiful white Wholecloths of intricate design and pattern? Such diary entries, indeed any documentary evidences relating to quilting, are so rare from this period that we may simply never know.

It was also in Allendale that the earliest surviving Strippy quilt from the North of England is known to have been made (fig 22).[10] Seamed in cotton prints and filled with fine wool, this strikingly coloured quilt could well owe its survival to having been taken to America when its owner emigrated in 1854. Thus it survived as a family treasure when the fate of most Strippy quilts, the least valued of all the North Country quilt types, was to be destroyed or discarded after use.

This particular quilt is of especial interest because it is also the earliest known example of the Strip quilting design, in which the quilting patterns are arranged in rows down the length of the quilt. The relative simplicity with which this design could be planned and stitched ensured its popularity in the later nineteenth century, mainly on Strippy quilts, but on Wholecloth quilts too (figs 47, 48 and 49). As a clear North Country characteristic, it is presumed to have evolved in this region, and is found surprisingly rarely elsewhere.

From the middle of the nineteenth century onwards quilt fashions changed, with a decline in Scrap quilts accompanied by a rise in Pieced and Appliqué quilts worked in a more restricted colour palette. Two-colour Block quilts, red, green and white Appliqué quilts and increasing numbers of Strippy quilts suggest a change to bought rather than found fabrics for quiltmaking. In other words, North Country quilters were now purchasing fabric for quilts and not simply relying on bits and pieces in the scrap bag. Indeed, from this time onwards it is doubtful if North Country quilts were ever made mostly from recycled materials.

FOCUS: JOSEPH HEDLEY OF WARDEN, NORTHUMBERLAND

The legend of 'Joe the Quilter', as Joseph Hedley was known in his neighbourhood, has passed into quilting folklore. But it was the manner of his death – murdered by person or persons unknown – which ensured his place in history. For he was killed on the night of January 3rd 1826 at Homers House, his lonely cottage on a quiet country road. A sad end for a man of 76. Were it not for his violent end, Joe's life would have passed, as did those of other quilters, leaving little trace.

Born in 1750, he became a tailor by trade and subsequently turned to quilting. He acquired a reputation for making fine quilts, working the Tynedale area as an itinerant quilter. He was also rumoured to be a man of means and it seems he was killed by a thief intent on stealing his money.

Fig 4 Joe Hedley's cottage at Homers Lane, Warden

But Joe was a poor man, receiving relief from the parish and gifts of food from neighbours to help him out. They knew he had spent many years nursing his bed-ridden wife Isabel, much older than he, who died in 1817 aged 96.[11]

Fig 3 Broadsheet on Joe Hedley's murder in 1826

Joe's murder shocked the neighbourhood, for he was a well-regarded man:

He was quite a genius in his line, and the taste which he displayed in the invention of his figures, and the care and dispatch with which he drew them, were very astonishing. He was ... one of the most harmless and inoffensive men... and always a welcome guest in every family in which he was employed ...[12]

The awful murder was never properly solved, though a vagrant in Carlisle did confess to the crime on his deathbed ten years later (1836).[13] A handful of quilts survive in museum collections which are said to have been made by him. With one exception, they are Wholecloth quilts of varying quality – and anecdotal evidence is their only connection to this famed quilter. Would that we could be sure that all were from his hand!

Fig 5 Detail of fig 18

Fig 6 *Framed Centre Medallion coverlet*
Made by Sarah Firth, a Quaker, of Huddersfield, Yorkshire
1783 (signed and dated)
Pieced, block-printed cottons and cotton broderie perse appliqué on linen
Unquilted
210 cm x 257 cm (82.5 x 101 inches)
Collection: The Bowes Museum, Barnard Castle, Co. Durham

Fig 7 *Framed Centre Medallion coverlet* (unfinished)
Made by Martha Jackson, probably in Westmorland
c. 1790–1795
Printed and white cottons, pieced and appliquéd, no backing
Unquilted
270 cm x 270 cm (106.5 x 106.5 inches)
On loan to Tullie House Museum, Carlisle

Fig 8 *Framed Diamond in the Square quilt* (centre detail)
Maker unknown, provenance probably Weardale
c. 1820-1840
Cotton fabrics
Bordered quilting design with stylized Leaf motifs; Geometric border patterns; and Wave filling
250 cm x 270 cm (98.5 x 106 inches)
Collection: Beamish: The North of England Open Air Museum, Co. Durham

Fig 9 *Framed Centre Medallion quilt* (centre detail)
Made by Mary Coatsworth, aged 15, of Middleton in Teesdale, Co. Durham
1817 (signed and dated)
White and printed cottons
Embroidered, and quilted following piecing
235 cm x 242 cm (92.5 x 95 inches)
Collection: The Bowes Museum, Barnard Castle, Co. Durham

Fig 11 *Framed Centre Medallion quilt* (centre detail)
Made by Elizabeth Norman of Lowick, Northumberland
c. 1810-1820, outer border added c.1850
Pieced in cotton chintz panels and framed in cotton chintzes, reverse white cotton
Bordered quilting design with Clamshell centre, and Cable Twist and Wavy Line borders
241 cm x 282 cm (95 x 112.5 inches)
Collection: The Bowes Museum, Barnard Castle, Co. Durham

Fig 10 *Framed Diamond in the Square*
Maker unknown, Cargo, nr. Carlisle, Cumberland
c. 1810-1840
Printed cottons, reverse white cotton
Allover quilting design in Wave pattern
250 cm x 252 cm (98.5 x 99 inches)
Private collection

NORTH COUNTRY QUILTS: LEGEND AND LIVING TRADITION

Fig 12 *Framed Diamond in the Square quilt*
Made by Miss Dickinson of Kidburngill, Lamplugh, Cumberland
c. 1850
Printed cottons, reverse white cotton
Allover quilting design in Wave pattern
301 cm x 306 cm (118 x 120.5 inches)
Collection: Tullie House Museum, Carlisle

INDUSTRIAL REVOLUTION AND COTTONS GALORE

Fig 13 *Framed Centre Medallion quilt*

Made at Carrig Rig Farm, Teesdale

c. 1850

Cotton fabrics, centre of pieced star and nine-patch blocks, reverse white linen, piped edge

Bordered quilting design includes Four-petalled Flowers in centre blocks; Wave, Chain and Cable Twist borders

235 cm x 239 cm (92.5 x 94 inches)

Collection: The Bowes Museum, Barnard Castle, Co. Durham

INDUSTRIAL REVOLUTION AND COTTONS GALORE

Fig 15 *Pieced quilt*
Possibly made by Annie Heslop as a wedding quilt, Walbottle, Northumberland
c. 1825
Multi-coloured cotton chintzes in pieced squares, white cotton back
Quilted in a design of squares with Lovers' Knot and Fan centre, Rose, Star, Square Diamonds and flower patterns within the squares
260 cm x 268 cm (102 x 106 inches)
Collection: Beamish: The North of England Open Air Museum, Co. Durham

Fig 14 *Framed Diamond in the Square/Pieced quilt* (detail, opposite left)
Made at Snow Field Farm, Stanhope, Weardale
c. 1835-1850
Pieced in a range of 1830s cotton dress fabrics
Bordered/allover quilting design with Wineglass and Clamshell centre set in an allover design of Wavy Line with Star and Four-petalled Flower; outer Wave border
243 cm x 254 cm (95.5 x 100 inches)
Collection: The Bowes Museum, Barnard Castle, Co. Durham

Fig 16 *Pieced Block quilt – Basket* (detail)
Maker unknown, Cumberland
1820-1840
Printed cottons, reverse white linen, pieced blocks and alternating large squares set 'on point'
Allover quilting design in Clamshell pattern
211 cm x 230 cm (83 x 90.5 inches)
Collection: The Bowes Museum, Barnard Castle, Co. Durham

NORTH COUNTRY QUILTS: LEGEND AND LIVING TRADITION

INDUSTRIAL REVOLUTION AND COTTONS GALORE

Fig 18 *Wholecloth quilt*

Made by Joseph Hedley of Warden, Northumberland

c. 1800-1826

Wool, probably homespun and home dyed

Bordered quilting design with Leaf and Flower motifs; Cable Twist and Geometric border patterns; Clamshell, Wave and Square Diamond fillers

200 cm x 228 cm (78.5 x 90 inches)

Collection: Tullie House Museum, Carlisle

Fig 17 *Pieced Block quilt – Single Irish Chain*
(detail, opposite left)

Made at Snow Field Farm, Stanhope, Weardale

c. 1830

Printed cottons with cream cotton back, piped edges

Quilted in the blocks with Four-petalled Flower, Rose, Heart, and Divided Circle motifs

222 cm x 248 cm (87.5 x 97.5 inches)

Collection: The Bowes Museum, Barnard Castle, Co. Durham

Fig 19 *Wholecloth quilt*

Made by Joseph Hedley of Warden, Northumberland

1824 (inscribed, "This was made by old Joe the Quilter in 1824…")

White linen, reverse white linen, cotton fringe added later

Bordered quilting design with floral centre, flower baskets and sprays; Running Feather, and Hammock with Shell borders

259 cm x 244 cm (102 x 96 inches)

Collection: The Bowes Museum, Barnard Castle, Co. Durham

Fig 20 *Wholecloth quilt*
Made by a member of the Murray family of Allendale, Northumberland
c. 1850
White cotton, top and reverse
Bordered quilting design with Flower Basket centre; Oval Leaf, Running Feather, Hammock with Daisy borders; Square Diamond filler
245 cm x 256 cm (96.5 x 101 inches)
Collection: The Bowes Museum, Barnard Castle, Co. Durham

INDUSTRIAL REVOLUTION AND COTTONS GALORE

Fig 21 *Pieced and Appliquéd quilt*
Made by Rebecca Temperley, probably in Allendale
c. 1860 (possibly for Rebecca's wedding)
Printed and white cottons, reverse white cotton
Bordered quilting design includes Clamshell, Wave, Cable Twist, and Geometric border with Roses
274 cm x 274 cm (108 x 108 inches)
Collection: The Bowes Museum, Barnard Castle, Co. Durham

Fig 22 *Strippy quilt* (detail)
Made by Hannah Peart (later Hannah Peart Graham) of Swinhope, Allendale, Northumberland
c. 1850 (Hannah emigrated to New York State in 1854 taking the quilt)
Printed cottons, white cotton back
Strip quilting design in Clamshell, Wavy Line and Geometric border patterns
183 cm x 234 cm (72 x 92 inches)
Collection: Killhope Lead Mining Centre, Upper Weardale, Co. Durham

1870~1918
A Golden Age and a Sewing Revolution

It was in this late nineteenth century/early twentieth century period that probably the greatest variety of North Country quilts were produced. Wholecloth quilts, the form which was to predominate in the twentieth century, appeared in ever-increasing numbers alongside Framed quilts and Block quilts, both Pieced and Appliquéd, together with the everyday Strippy. Vitality and charm are the essence of the best quilts from this era, some of which are so individual in character as to defy categorization (fig 54).

Why was this such a golden age for North Country quilting? As a traditional practice firmly established in the North of England in the earlier part of the nineteenth century, it had become part of the vernacular regional culture. Once particular patterns and designs were identified with the region, it seems that they were used with conscious pride. Quiltmaking became a means of expressing a regional identity, probably as important as any aesthetic intent on the part of the maker. Firmly established as a regional cultural practice, it remained resistant to the dictates of high fashion and metropolitan influence up until the First World War.

The ongoing community role of quiltmaking also contributed as families and friends continued to 'twilt' together around the frame (fig 23), whilst social gatherings which combined quiltmaking with music, song and dance continued much as before. Writing in 1950 of his childhood in the dales, one Weardale man remembered:

To go prossing (chatting) to each other's houses was almost a regular thing ... should a quilt be in the making (and what pieces of art they were, both in design and work, especially the patchwork ones) with two or three quilters helping them the talk would be a little harmless gossip on the ordinary doings of village life or, if some scandal got on the wing, their voices would sink to a whisper and heads draw a little closer lest the bairns should hear.[1]

Another social factor was competitive pressure. Intense rivalry developed between quilters, especially in the North Pennine Dales, helping to maintain a high standard of workmanship and design. Later, as agricultural shows included craft sections, quilts were placed in open competition. One Allendale lady remembered, 'those [quilts] done for shows had to be done a very fine pattern, tiny little [square] diamonds and the pattern had to be very close'.[2]

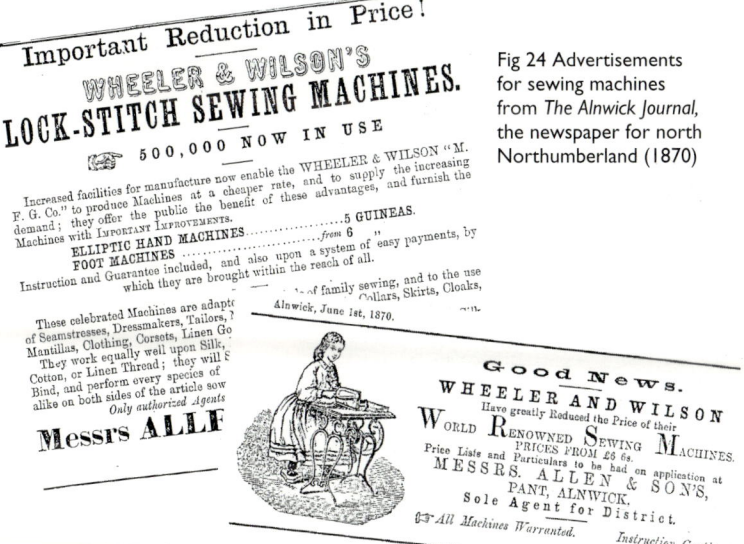

Fig 24 Advertisements for sewing machines from *The Alnwick Journal*, the newspaper for north Northumberland (1870)

The invention of the sewing machine may also have played a part. The first practical domestic sewing machine was patented in 1851 by Isaac M. Singer of Pittstown, New York. Other manufacturers soon followed to produce what became the first domestic 'consumer appliance'.[3] Ten years later, sewing machines could readily be purchased in Newcastle, North East England's main retail centre. By 1870 sewing machines could not only be purchased but hired on a weekly basis in smaller towns around the region.[4]

Fig 23 *The Wedding Quilt* by renowned local artist Ralph Hedley, 1883 (private collection)

So, by the end of the nineteenth century, sewing machines had become commonplace in homes and were used for quiltmaking as well as for dressmaking. Though the machine could not replicate a hand stitched quilting line, and few quilters attempted to make it do so, it could speed up the process of preparing a quilt top. For certain styles of pieced quilt, Framed quilts in particular, the hand stitched technique previously used for seaming pieces was easily translated to the machine. But it was the comparative ease with which lengths of fabric for Wholecloth and Strippy quilts could be 'run up' on the machine that made it an ideal tool for seaming these particular quilt tops – perhaps one reason why their popularity increased so dramatically.

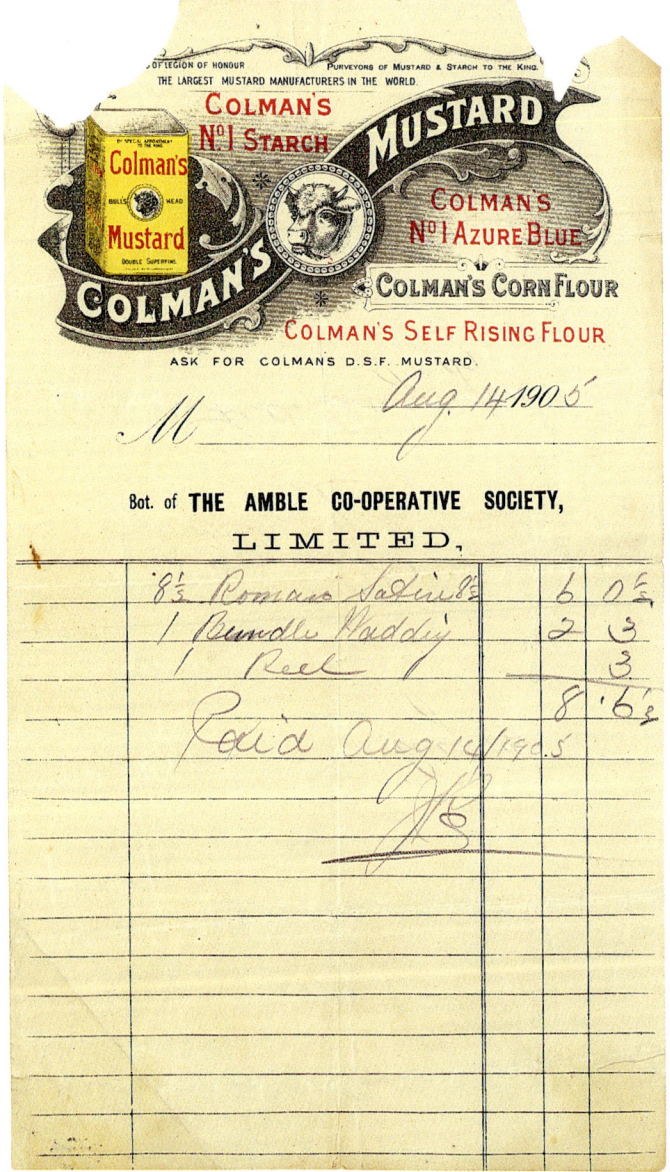

Fig 25 Bill for fabrics bought by Mrs Shepherd of Amble (1905) who ran a 'quilt club' after a mining accident left her husband unable to work. The 8½ yard length of 'Roman Satin' (sateen) would have been divided into three and seamed together for a quilt top; the cost per yard was 8½d (c. 3p).

Nor were fabrics difficult to obtain. Inexpensive cottons, at as little as 3d (1.25p) per yard,[5] could be purchased from town and village drapers, travelling salesmen or from the local market. Another major supplier was the local 'Co-op'. Every town had its own Co-operative Society which catered for just about everything - and paid 'divi' (a percentage dividend on spend) as well. It was the local Co-op that became the main supplier of cotton wadding (bought in rolls to be fluffed up by the fire) which, by this period, had largely replaced wool as a filling, though occasionally an old blanket was used instead.

As new fabrics became available, they too could be adapted to quiltmaking. The late nineteenth century vogue for Turkey red fabrics, colourfast and produced for a variety of domestic and clothing items, led to the fashion for Turkey red and white quilts. As in other parts of Britain, North Country quilters quickly took to the dramatic colour combination of red and white, in sharp contrast to their more usual pastel tones. Red and white Block quilts and Framed quilts appeared (fig 39) but most popular of all was the Turkey red and white Strippy (fig 40).

The increasing trend towards Wholecloth quilts also had an effect on fabric choice. Though the all-white, fine cotton quilt remained a perennial favourite, an increasing trend towards using fabrics with a sheen, to accentuate quilting design, led to the widespread adoption of furnishing sateen for Wholecloth quilts. Sufficiently lightweight for hand quilting, cotton sateen produced a handsome quilt and became almost universally adopted for this quilt type by the early twentieth century. Flowered sateen also made an appearance as the border fabric in Framed Wholecloth quilts (fig 42).

On Strippy quilts, patterned cottons gradually gave way to plain (unprinted) fabrics, or to a simple combination of a patterned with a plain cotton. Cotton sateens were introduced into Strippy quilts as well as Wholecloths, particularly after the turn of the twentieth century. But the Strippy quilt in fig 45, pieced in wool fabrics, is a rare type.

Wool quilts in general are comparatively uncommon. Other North Country examples are known, pieced from suiting samples, but the Wholecloth quilts in figs 47, 48 and 49 appear to be a specific north Northumberland type - wool quilts, made from probably homespun yarn then mill woven cloth, and quilted with a Strip quilting design. Local folk lore suggests that farmers from this area sent wool to the nearby mills at Otterburn and Tosson to be dyed and woven into cloth for family use.

So this association of factors - regional culture, social influences and pressures, fabric availability, and the speed and practicalities of a new stitching revolution - combined to maintain and enhance the vitality of North Country quilting. Nowhere was this more evident than in the North Pennine Dales. Always a nineteenth century quilting 'hotspot', it was into this region that American influences were absorbed with evident enthusiasm. The vibrant Appliqué quilts in figs 50 and 51 appear to be copies of American quilts of the same genre; only their quilting designs remain characteristically North Country. In similar vein, traditional American pieced blocks such as the Feathered Star in fig 56 appeared, particularly on dales' quilts, but with regional quilting designs superimposed on the Pieced Block design. The assumption must be that emigrés sent American piecing and appliqué patterns to relatives back home, but there are no real hard evidences.

Though quiltmaking remained a home based activity, it continued to provide opportunity for income. One group of women who began to make quilts for a living were those whose husbands had been killed or injured in pit accidents – an all to frequent occurrence. In the mining villages of Northumberland and Durham many women in such circumstances ran a quilt 'club', whereby a number of customers paid a small weekly sum, usually 1 shilling, for a number of weeks until the full cost of a quilt was paid.[6] The weekly income financed material costs and gave the quilter a small profit. The customers received a quilt in turn, often drawing lots to decide the order of receipt.

The quilt 'club' was thus a type of credit club. Wholecloth and Strippy quilts in cotton sateen were their stock in trade and quilts were completed, on average, every two to three weeks which necessarily limited their design. Large repeated motifs in simple Bordered or Strip forms make up the quilting designs on most of these 'club' quilts but, despite the pressure of circumstance under which they were made, some have a quality and integrity of purpose which transcends the somewhat restricted nature of their origins.

The earliest recorded quilt 'club' began in 1870 and the 'club' system continued for another 40 years. Researching in the 1950s for her classic book *Traditional Quilting*,[7] Mavis FitzRandolph met many women of the following generation whose mothers had run such 'clubs':

Mrs. J. Hitchcock, whose mother, a widow with six children, started her club about 1890, recalled that wages were paid fortnightly and so the club contributions were similarly collected, but weekly collection seems to have been more usual. Two shillings was the weekly instalment in a Tweedmouth club between the wars, but one shilling was more often mentioned, or sometimes "one or two shillings a week". Mrs. Graham started her club when her widowed mother-in-law came to live with her; there were several children and only small wages coming in; they made a total of two hundred quilts ... one quilter enrolled forty members, another boasted: "Ma mither had the roon of the place for quilts".[8]

Later oral history researchers recorded other daughters and granddaughters of these 'club' quilters with poignant memories of the hardships endured.[9]

A second group of professionals emerged, also around the 1880s. Known in the region as 'quilt stampers', the quilt designers of the North Pennine Dales marked out designs for quilting onto fabric that either they, or their customers, had purchased. An account of the trade and its chief practitioners is given in the Focus pages overleaf.[10]

The evolution of this service trade was to have a profound influence on North Country quilting design in the twentieth century. Its initial effect was to change the nature of design on Wholecloth quilts, the quilt type which became the designers' main product. Up to the late nineteenth century, the Wholecloth quilt surface was still usually divided into areas (centres, borders and corners) by double or triple lines of quilting, which were then filled with the quilter's choice of patterns. The quilt designers dropped these separating lines and allowed patterns to 'flow' together. They also developed very large central designs, packed with a variety of repeated patterns, which extended and often almost joined with the corners or borders (fig 55). This cut down the area of filling pattern which, though seemingly simple, is hard to mark and time-consuming to stitch.

The result of these changes was a form of design which was far more fluid and dramatic but still essentially practical. Its popularity was assured and the effect of this new style of large-centred, flowing design can increasingly be 'read' in North Country Wholecloth quilts right through to the end of the twentieth century.

Focus: Allenheads and the Quilt Design Trade

In the two North Pennine Dales of Allendale and Weardale, a unique trade evolved in the latter part of the nineteenth century, and continued for many years with a peak around 1910. A handful of individuals, most trained by apprenticeship, set up in business marking out quilting designs onto quilt tops. They were known in the area as quilt 'stampers', though they did not 'stamp out' their designs but drew them onto fabric with a blue coloured pencil.

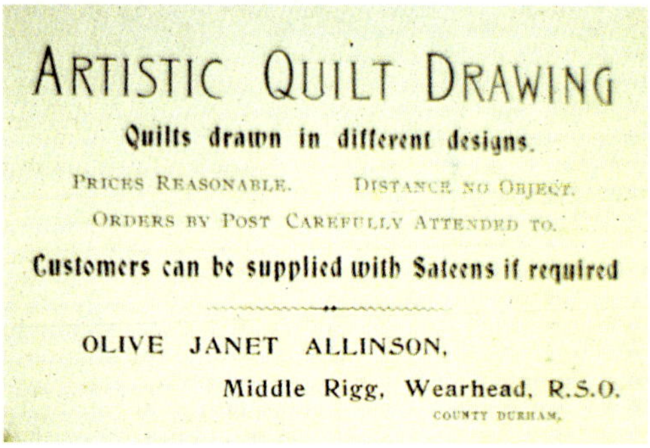

Fig 26 Business card circulated (c. 1915) by Olive Allinson, a quilt designer of Wearhead, Upper Weardale, and the only designer known to have advertised in this way; she later married and became Mrs Heatherington

The quilt designers worked to order, with customers requesting a particular type of quilt top in a particular colour to be dispatched by post, or sending their own ready-seamed fabric top for marking. Costs for marking only were very modest – 1/6d (7½p) was the standard charge until the 1930s. The designers also made up quilt tops 'on spec' which were either sold direct to customers, or collected by 'packmen' and taken for sale around the farmhouses and cottages of northern England.

Fig 27 Allenheads village (c. 1910) from below the village school; apart from the wooden mining shaft tower (centre), the scene is little changed today

Customers who bought a quilt top added their own backing and filling and simply stitched along the marked lines to produce a stunningly beautiful quilt – for the quilt designers achieved a quality in their designs rarely matched since. Using a combination of pattern templates and freehand drawing, they produced intricate designs that are quite unique in style. Though they worked to standard layout plans, the designers used a characteristic set of patterns – some of which can be regarded as 'trademarks' for they are found only on these designed quilts. So a quilt of this kind from the North Pennine Dales can be clearly identified – even if it turns up on the other side of the world!

Fig 28 Lead mine in Allenheads (c. 1910)

Most of the quilt tops marked out in this way were Wholecloth ones but the designers seamed and marked out Strippy tops and Star tops too. They also drew designs onto Pieced and Appliquéd tops made up by customers (fig 54) which were sent and returned by post. Though never formally advertised, the service provided by the quilt designers was popular with both individual quilters and quilting groups, especially in North East England. Even professional 'club' quilters in mining villages, who quilted for a living, were known to purchase a designed quilt top for a special family quilt.

Just why did this singular trade evolve in this remote part of Britain? That – the big question – is now addressed.

A GOLDEN AGE AND A SEWING REVOLUTION

FOCUS:
GEORGE GARDINER AND ELIZABETH SANDERSON OF ALLENHEADS, NORTHUMBERLAND

These two legendary figures, both from the village of Allenheads, were the chief protagonists of the quilt design trade. George, an Allenheads shop-keeper, is thought to have started the business from his little drapery shop on the edge of the village, probably in the 1880s.[11] Elizabeth was apprenticed to him and subsequently established her own home-based business.

Born around 1853, George was raised by his grandmother. Unlike most men of the village, he did not take up employment in the lead mining industry. Instead he became a draper and married Sarah, a milliner from a village a mile or so down the dale. In the 1870s they set up home at Smelt Mill Cottages and, presumably together, ran a drapery and millinery business.

Fig 30 Detail of quilt in fig 55

Her reputation was widespread and she, in turn, taught other young girls, some of whom walked six miles over the hill tops from Weardale each week and stayed in the Sanderson home as 'live-in' apprentices.[12] She was never short of work, always with a pile of cotton sateen waiting to be seamed and marked and her workroom produced hundreds of quilt tops over the years. Many survive identified by their blue pencil lines, characteristic patterns and quality designs. But only a mere handful can be certainly ascribed to Elizabeth's hand – for these quilts were never signed.

The unique style of these designed quilts seems to have been set at the very outset when the trade was first established. The style is so individual, with its use of large centres, flowing borders and characteristic patterns – somewhat different to earlier North Country quilts. So who set this style? Was it George Gardiner? More than likely, but what is certain is that Elizabeth Sanderson had a subsequent influence in developing distinctive new quilt tops – like the Sanderson Star.

Fig 29 Elizabeth Sanderson (right) and two apprentices (in doorway) outside her home and workshop at Fawside Green, Allenheads (c. 1910)

How and why did this village draper come to establish this quilt design trade? The answer probably lies in the economic changes of the time. Allenheads was utterly dependent on the fortunes of the lead mining industry. In the latter half on the nineteenth century, the price of lead slumped and the industry declined. Families left the dales in search of other work with a consequent effect on village trade. Perhaps George Gardiner began designing quilt tops in an effort to keep his business alive. If so, it appears to have been successful for he apprenticed several young women.

Elizabeth Sanderson, one of these apprentices, set up her own workroom at home in Fawside Green, designing and marking out quilt tops until her death in 1933 at the age of 72.

What is also certain is that these two individuals were the prime influences in a trade which produced some outstanding North Country quilts.

Fig 31 Detail of quilt in fig 69

A GOLDEN AGE AND A SEWING REVOLUTION

Fig 33 *Framed Diamond in the Square quilt - with Flowerpot appliqué*

Made by Isabella Cruddas of Rookhope, Weardale

c. 1880

White and green cotton with Turkey red print, reverse white cotton

Bordered quilting design with centre of Square Diamond filler with Rose motif; Chain, Cable Twist, and Wavy Line borders

234 cm x 234 cm (92 x 92 inches)

Collection: Beamish: The North of England Open Air Museum, Co. Durham

Fig 34 *Pieced Block quilt - Single Irish Chain* (detail)

Made by Phoebe Jane Lister of Consett, then Frosterley, Co. Durham

c. 1870-1880

Turkey red cotton print and white cotton, white cotton reverse

Quilted to link with the pieced blocks with Heart, Star and Diamond motifs; Chain and Wave borders

232 cm x 252 cm (91 x 99 inches)

Private collection

Fig 32 *Framed quilt*

Maker unknown, provenance probably Cumberland

c. 1840-1910

Floral cotton prints with commemorative block centre - to the Friendly Association of Cotton Spinners (1806-1838). Top includes late eighteenth century fabrics and others dating from the 1830s but machine pieced and finished; reverse early twentieth century flowered furnishing cotton

Allover quilting design in Wave pattern

252 cm x 252 cm (99 x 99 inches)

Collection: Tullie House Museum, Carlisle

Fig 35 *Pieced Block quilt - Eight-pointed Star*
Maker unknown, provenance Pity Me, Co. Durham
c. 1880
Green and white cotton
Quilting follows pieced blocks with Diamond and Rose motifs, a Four-petalled Flower motif in the centre; Square Diamond filler
221 cm x 226 cm (87 x 89 inches)
Collection: Beamish: The North of England Open Air Museum, Co. Durham

A GOLDEN AGE AND A SEWING REVOLUTION

Fig 36 *Pieced Block quilt - Jockey Cap*
Made by a member of the Roddam family, Wolf Cleugh, Weardale, Co. Durham
c. 1890-1910
Pink and white cotton, white cotton reverse
Quilting follows pieced blocks with Four-petalled Flower motif, concentric circles; Diamond filler and Curved Feather border
187 cm x 227 cm (73.5 x 98.5 inches)
Collection: The Bowes Museum, Barnard Castle, Co. Durham

Fig 37 *Framed quilt/Strippy quilt*
Maker and provenance unknown
c. 1890
Two cotton prints with blue cotton, reverse in printed and plain Turkey red cotton strips
Bordered quilting design with central Oval Leaf motifs; Cable Twist, Feathered, Geometric, and Wavy Line borders
203 cm x 244 cm (80 x 96 inches)
Collection: The Bowes Museum, Barnard Castle, Co. Durham

A GOLDEN AGE AND A SEWING REVOLUTION

Fig 38 *Pieced Block quilt - Single Irish Chain and Diamond in the Square - with appliqué centre*
Maker unknown, made for Ruth Watson (née Kipling) of Tow Law, Co. Durham, for her wedding
c. 1888
Printed and plain cottons, reverse white cotton, bound edge
Quilting design follows pieced blocks with outline quilting and assorted motifs in the blocks; Rose with Wave border
254 cm x 254 cm (100 x 100 inches)
Collection: The Bowes Museum, Barnard Castle, Co. Durham

Fig 39 *Framed Diamond in the Square quilt*

Maker unknown, belonged to Mary Ann Parkin of Middleton in Teesdale, Co. Durham

c. 1880-1900

Turkey red and white cottons, reverse white cotton

Bordered quilting design with centre of Four-petalled Flower, Square Diamond filler and corner Roses; Wineglass, Wave, Cable Twist and Curved Line borders

221 cm x 227 cm (87 x 89.5 inches)

Collection: The Bowes Museum, Barnard Castle, Co. Durham

Fig 40 *Strippy quilt* (detail)

Maker possibly Mrs Young of Battersby, near Great Ayton, North Yorkshire

c. 1890

Turkey red and white cotton twill, reverse in Turkey red cotton

Strip quilting design with Wavy Line, Four-petalled Flower, and Cable border patterns

198 cm x 210 cm (78 x 82.5 inches)

Collection: The Bowes Museum, Barnard Castle, Co. Durham

Fig 41 *Wholecloth quilt* (detail)

Made by Susan Southgate, nanny to the Baker-Baker family of Elemore Hall, near Easington, County Durham. She made one quilt for each child in her care.

1890s

White cotton, top and reverse

Bordered quilting design with central circular motif including Scrolls and corner Fans; Plait, Chain and Scrolled Wreath borders; Diamond and Square Diamond filler

235 cm x 245 cm (92.5 x 96.5 inches)

Private collection

Fig 42 *Framed Wholecloth quilt*

Maker and provenance unknown

c. 1890

Printed and plain ('old gold') cotton sateen, reverse deep pink cotton

Bordered quilting design with large centre of Fans inside a Feather Wreath; Feathered and Cable Twist borders; Square Diamond filler

204 cm x 242 cm (80 x 95 inches)

Collection: The Bowes Museum, Barnard Castle, Co. Durham

Fig 43 *Strippy quilt* (detail)

Maker unknown, provenance probably Tynedale

c.1870

Printed cottons

Strip quilting design with Running Feather and looped leaves border patterns with Square Diamond filler

211 cm x 254 cm (83 x 100 inches)

Collection: Beamish: The North of England Open Air Museum, Co. Durham

A GOLDEN AGE AND A SEWING REVOLUTION

Fig 44 *Strippy quilt*
Maker's name unknown, made in Wearhead, Weardale, Co. Durham
c. 1880-1900
Turkey red and dark cream cottons
Strip quilting design with Hammock, Wineglass, Diamond Twist, Oval and Four-petalled Flower border patterns
209 cm x 222 cm (82 x 87.5 inches)
Collection: Beamish: The North of England Open Air Museum, Co. Durham

Fig 45 *Pieced Strippy quilt* (detail)
Maker unknown, provenance probably Tynedale
1880-1900
Wool and cotton fabrics
Strip quilting design with Cable Twist border pattern and Rose motifs
243 cm x 234 cm (95.5 x 92 inches)
Collection: The Quilters' Guild of the British Isles

Fig 46 *Strippy quilt* (detail)
Maker unknown, possibly designed by a quilt designer
c. 1910
Pink and white cottons, reverse flowered cotton twill
Strip quilting design with Open Flower, Weardale Chain, Rose with freehand stem and scrolls, and Plait border patterns
210 cm x 230 cm (82.5 x 90.5 inches)
Collection: The Quilters' Guild of the British Isles

Fig 48 *Wholecloth quilt* (detail)

Made by a member of the Keith family, Elsdon, Northumberland

c. 1875-1900

Homespun wool (probably mill woven) top and reverse; top hand dyed, reverse natural wool (sister quilt to fig 47)

Strip quilting design with Cable Twist, and linked Circles with Oval Leaves

172 x 220 cm (69 x 86.5 inches)

Collection: The Bowes Museum, Barnard Castle, Co. Durham

Fig 47 *Wholecloth quilt* (opposite left)

Made by a member of the Keith family, Elsdon, Northumberland

c. 1875-1900

Homespun wool (probably mill woven) top and reverse, top hand dyed, reverse natural wool (sister quilt to fig 48)

Strip quilting design with Wavy Line and Geometric border patterns filled with Rose and Four-petalled Flower motifs; Diamond filler

182 x 232 cm (71.5 x 91 inches)

Collection: The Bowes Museum, Barnard Castle, Co. Durham

Fig 49 *Wholecloth quilt* (detail)

Maker unknown, provenance probably North Northumberland

c. 1875-1900

Wool, top and reverse

Strip quilting design with Wavy Line and Geometric borders filled with Heart and flower spray motifs; double Square Diamond filler

161 cm x 221 cm (63.5 x 87 inches)

Private collection

NORTH COUNTRY QUILTS: LEGEND AND LIVING TRADITION

Fig 50 *Appliqué Block quilt - Turkey Tracks - with Pieced border*
Maker probably Martha Metcalfe (née Dent), of Barnard Castle, before her marriage
c. 1880-1890
Red, white and green cottons, reverse white cotton
Quilted design follows blocks with Diamond motifs and Diamond filler; Diamond border pattern in sashing; Wave, Clamshell and Square Diamond outer border
234 cm x 237 cm (92 x 93.5 inches)
Collection: The Bowes Museum, Barnard Castle, Co. Durham

A GOLDEN AGE AND A SEWING REVOLUTION

Fig 51 *Framed quilt - Princess Feather appliquéd centre and Tree Everlasting pieced borders*
Made by a member of the Wood family, West Woodburn, Northumberland
c. 1870-1890
Pink and green cottons with white cotton twill, reverse white cotton twill
Bordered quilting design with Feather motifs in the centre applique; Wineglass, Chain, Rose and Goosewing borders; Square Diamond filler
238 cm x 241 cm (94 x 95 inches)
Collection: The Bowes Museum, Barnard Castle, Co. Durham

Fig 52 *Appliqué quilt - Princess Feather and Star*
Made by Mrs Goldsborough of Pelton, Co. Durham, for the wedding of Isabella Levitt
1895
Turkey red and white cotton, reverse white cotton
Strip quilting design with Fan, circles of Four-petalled Flowers, Running Feather, Worm and Plait border patterns
211 x 241 (83 x 95 inches)
Collection: Beamish: The North of England Open Air Museum, Co. Durham

Fig 53 *Framed Star quilt top* (detail, unfinished)

Pieced by Elizabeth Featherstone (later Mrs Coulthard of Cowshill, Weardale), quilting design drawn by Olive Allinson of Wearhead, Weardale (later Mrs Heatherington), apprenticed to Elizabeth Sanderson

1911-1914

Green and white cotton, marked with blue pencil

Bordered quilting design following piecing with large Rose centre and freehand patterns; Cable Twist and freehand feathered borders; outer border of Weardale Chain

237 cm x 237 cm (93.5 x 93.5 inches)

Collection: The Quilters' Guild of the British Isles

Fig 55 *Wholecloth quilt* (opposite right)

Made by Louise Rutherford of Rothbury, Northumberland, top designed by a quilt designer from Allendale, Northumberland

c. 1910

Cream cotton sateen, top and reverse

Bordered quilting design with centre of Feather Wreath, Feathers and Scroll motifs; Leaf, Fan and Scroll corner motifs; Goosewing with Rose and Scroll border patterns; Square Diamond filler

214 cm x 249 cm (84 x 98 inches)

Private collection

Fig 54 *Pieced quilt - Triple X* (detail)

Maker unknown, provenance probably Castleside, Co. Durham, quilting design probably marked out by a quilt designer

c. 1910

Yellow and cream cotton sateen, reverse flowered furnishing cotton

Bordered quilting design with Rose in a Ring, freehand Feathers, Small Feather, and Scroll motifs; Plait, Weardale Chain, and Cable Twist borders

226 cm x 241 cm (89 x 95 inches)

Collection: The Quilters' Guild of the British Isles

A GOLDEN AGE AND A SEWING REVOLUTION

Fig 56 *Pieced Block quilt - Feathered Star*
Maker unknown, provenance probably Allendale
c. 1890
Cotton chintz and white cotton, white cotton reverse
Allover quilting design of repeated motifs: Daisy in Eight-pointed Star patterns with Square Diamond filler
204 cm x 204 cm (80.5 x 80.5 inches)
Collection: Beamish: The North of England Open Air Museum, Co. Durham

1918~1939
POST-WAR CHANGES AND NEW PATRONAGE

During the First World War, many women's lives altered as they were brought directly into the war effort or had to adapt to a more independent role in family and society. This social change was accompanied by fashion and lifestyle changes, with women's magazines an important influence. Quilts were already falling out of use as bed covers, and fabrics were more difficult to obtain, so North Country quilting declined over most of the northern counties in the immediate post-war years. Only in areas where quilt 'clubs' and quilting groups were an established part of social practice was North Country quilting revived to any extent, and then just in North East England and the North Pennine Dales – the latter still a quilting 'hotspot'. To the west of the Pennines, it seems that few quilts were made after the First World War.

The 'clubs' run by women in mining villages, with their regular customers subscribing each week, thrived again at least through the 1920s, but the regular flow of customers may have had as much to do with altruism as with the practical need for a hand-stitched quilt. Close-knit communities remained willing to help a woman struggling to raise her family without a regular man's wage coming in – it was a way of 'helping out'.[1] In terms of design, the 'club quilt' was by now rarely anything other than a Wholecloth quilt, with large repeated motifs, mainly Roses and Feathers, worked into simple Bordered or Strip quilting designs. With a limited pattern stock and rather stiff designs, most 'club quilts' of this era have a somewhat formal and rigid appearance, though one 'club' quilter, Mrs Shepherd of Amble, Northumberland, did produce some stunning quilts, carefully crafting her own patterns and design formats (fig 63).

Quilting provided another opportunity for community self-help in this same Northumberland coal-shipping port, as Mavis FitzRandolph recorded:

The quilt frame, in fact, seems to have taken the place now held by the whist drive as a money-raiser. Amble's (Northumberland) war memorial (1918) was provided by a tremendous communal quilt-making effort by every denomination; about a hundred quilts were finally displayed in the village hall and the fact that there were so many shows the popularity of the work at that time.[2]

FitzRandolph goes on to record that:

Several North Country Women's Institutes raised funds for themselves in their early days by raffling quilts which were worked on by members co-operatively. This idea became so popular at one time that a group of Hexhamshire members decided to make one, even though none of them felt equal to designing it. They got a pattern drawn on paper by a Durham woman ...[3]

And referring again to the Amble quilts:

When the various church quilt clubs in Amble were working hard to raise funds ... they took a lot of their material to the stores [shop] to be sent away to be marked, "otherwise they would never have got them done in time"...[4]

These anecdotes highlight a growing problem within the North Country quiltmaking tradition at this time – the decline in design standards and loss of design skills. Design for quilting had gradually 'loosened' over the last quarter of the nineteenth century; the reliance on using the resource of a quilt designer had increased; and the hard won oral knowledge and collective wisdom of pattern stock and pattern use were no longer being passed down the generations. Even the simpler and bolder forms of piecing and appliqué, seen on North Country quilts of the previous century, were dropped in favour of piecing hexagons together from fabric scraps.

Fig 57 Hannah Petty of Nenthead, near Alston, Cumbria, the wife of the village schoolmaster, who had no family but made many quilts in her lifetime including the Wholecloth quilt in fig 65; she died aged 77 sometime in the 1930s

The result of these changes was that, by the 1920s, most North Country quilts still being made were Wholecloth ones, technically difficult, but produced either by professional 'club' quilters, by community effort, or designed by one or other of the still active quilt designers for customers to quilt. Rare examples of quilts designed and made by individual quilters in this period include figs 64 and 65; both are made from figured chintz and perhaps intended to replicate the look of an eiderdown and so to be more in keeping with the style of the time. Another 1920s vogue was for 'old gold' sateen, often combined with pink either in strippy quilts (fig 68) or for the two sides of a wholecloth quilt (fig 66).

The influence of the quilt designers continued to be wide reaching in North Country quilts of this period, at least up to the early 1930s. Working in both Weardale and Allendale, their stock in trade included not only Wholecloth quilts but Strippy quilts (fig 68) and Star quilts too (fig 69 and 70). The latter, today referred to as the 'Sanderson Star', is a unique North Country design; it was highly popular, with numerous examples of this dramatic, double-star, two-colour design having survived.

The quilt designers' quality of product remained as high as it had been in the pre-war era, at least until the death of Elizabeth Sanderson in 1933. Although design was recognizably formulaic, the number and variety of patterns used and the quality of the pattern line drawn onto the quilt tops continued to provide customers with designs that they themselves could not equal. Little wonder so many individual quilters took the easy route and ordered a quilt top from a designer or bought one from a packman. Only their stitching skills were then required to produce a handsome quilt:

...the custom of buying drawn quilt tops, or of sending one's own material away to be marked, spread to such an extent that a number of quilters never learnt to mark a pattern and cannot do so to this day. It had a stultifying effect on Northumberland and Durham designs.[5]

The communities in which the quilt designers lived also took advantage of their skills. The quilt tops in figs 71 and 72 were stitched together by family and community effort in the village of Carr Shield, not far from Allenheads, around 1930.[6] They then asked their near neighbour, Elizabeth Sanderson, to draft a quilting design for each quilt which she marked out in the characteristic blue pencil on coarse cotton backing. Unfortunately, the pieced nature of the quilt tops masks the stunning quilting designs, their unique

PRICES OF QUILTED WORK

PRICES vary according to the amount of work in the pattern and the materials used. The average prices per square foot, for large quilts, when there is no waste of material, are:

Sateen or fine cotton	3/8 per square foot
Fine cotton poplin	4/- per square foot
Shanghai silk	6/- per square foot

Estimates can be given for sizes and materials required. The following are specimen prices for standard sizes:

Silk Dressing Gowns, quilted all over, from	£8 8 0
Silk Dressing Jackets, quilted all over	£5 10 0
Silk Cushions, down filled, from	£1 18 6

Cot Quilts (about 3 ft. × 2 ft.):

Sateen or fine cotton, from	£1 5 0
Poplin	£1 8 6
Silk	£2 2 0

Quilts for single beds:

Eiderdown size (about 5 ft. × 4 ft.)

Sateen or fine cotton	£3 15 0
Silk	£5 10 0

Counterpane size (about 6 ft. × 7 ft.)

Sateen or fine cotton	£7 7 0
Poplin	£8 8 0
Silk	£11 11 0

Fig 58 Price list produced by the Rural Industries Bureau for their quilts, cushions and quilted garments sold in London galleries (1930s)

quality and originality bearing witness to the talents of a remarkable lady, if it was indeed Miss Sanderson who marked them.

Another remarkable lady – but one from far outwith the region – was Mavis FitzRandolph, the driving force behind an institutional scheme to revive quilting in the late 1920s and 1930s. The Rural Industries Bureau (RIB), based in London, attempted to revive rural crafts in 'distressed areas'.[7] Quilting was just one of these crafts and schemes were established in South Wales and County Durham whereby selected quilters were provided with all the necessary materials to produce quilts for the London market. Only quality materials were used, silk or top quality cotton sateen or poplin; wool for wadding, traditionally used in Wales (but not then in the North of England) was also supplied.

Using patterns characteristic of each area, the distinctive quilts produced were referred to as 'Welsh' quilts and 'Durham' quilts, respectively.

In order to recruit enough quilters in Wales, classes were established where young girls were taught both design skills and stitching techniques; in County Durham, Mavis FitzRandolph recruited older women who had quilted either for their own family use or had run quilt 'clubs'. She later wrote, "the county federation of Women's Institutes was in touch with good quilters in the pit villages, of whom we chose the neediest",[8] a clear recognition of the organizer's sense of social, as well as craft, responsibilities.

The Durham quilters drew on their own individual skills and drafted rather formal layouts using the, by now standard, North Country Feathers and Roses. The quilts marketed under the scheme were all Wholecloth ones but a new line was also introduced – quilted clothing. Echoing the fashion two centuries before, jackets, dressing gowns and baby's matinee sets were designed and made up – and proved very popular.

The RIB scheme was an undoubted success with highlights including an order from no less an institution than Claridge's Hotel in London:

Quilt wives in South Wales and County Durham have been chosen to make bed coverlets ... for the new wing of Claridge's Hotel ... some fifty women have taken part ... many of the County Durham quilters have worked in pairs at the frame to complete the orders in time.[9]

The scheme was regrettably brought to an abrupt end with the outbreak of war in 1939. But there had been a significant regional spin-off – the introduction of the Northern Industries Workrooms (NIW) scheme (see Focus page overleaf).

Patronage had also came from another institutional source – the National Federation of Women's Institutes (WI). Part of the National Federation's educational remit was to encourage domestic skills and traditional crafts and, in the mid 1920s, they appointed Alice Armes as Handicrafts Advisor, herself a native of County Durham. Both patchwork and quilting were encouraged and featured in the National Federation Exhibitions of 1932 and 1936. One north country visitor was quoted as saying: "Queer how much store the folks down here set on our quilts. We think them just ordinary".[10]

The local WI Federations of Northumberland and Durham also played their part in promoting North Country quilting. Like the National Federation, they introduced classes for quilting in handicraft shows and organized exhibitions; the exquisite little cot quilt in fig 77 was first exhibited in the 1930s at The Bowes Museum and subsequently acquired for its collections.

As with the RIB and NIW schemes, the momentum built up by the Women's Institutes to revive the declining craft of quilting was brought to an abrupt halt with the outbreak of war. But a lasting legacy of this inter-war period is the appellation 'Durham quilt' for a quilt in North Country style. Quite how it evolved is a mystery. It may have come from the term used by the London galleries to distinguish their quilts made in County Durham from those produced in South Wales. Equally, it may have been introduced by the WI.[11] Whatever the source, 'Durham quilting' became firmly entrenched in the quilting vocabulary and has remained there ever since.

FOCUS: THE NORTHERN INDUSTRIES WORKROOMS

Following the success of the Rural Industries Bureau scheme to regenerate quilting, the Northern Industries Workrooms (NIW) were established in County Durham. Unlike the Rural Industries Bureau scheme which used home-based workers, this Northern Industries scheme set up special places of work – the Workrooms – with employees to carry out orders for quilts and other products. Lady Cuthbert Headlam, wife of the Member of Parliament for Barnard Castle, was the driving force and two main centres were established – in Barnard Castle itself, and at Langley Moor near Durham City.

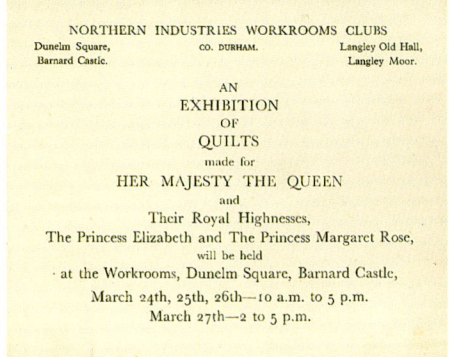

Fig 61 Invitation card to the NIW exhibition of royal quilts in Barnard Castle (1938)

Fig 59 The Northern Industries Workrooms' staff (1930s)

The Barnard Castle Workroom opened in 1933 and closed in the early years of the Second World War. The Workroom produced not only quilts but soft toys too and at its peak employed over twenty people – mostly girls and young women – a considerable boost to employment in the town.

Fig 60 Bill for a satin quilt of unknown size (1940)

The quilts produced were mainly small – cot sized or single bed sized – and all Wholecloth ones. The Workrooms used more high quality fabrics than had hitherto been the case for North Country quilts; out went everyday cottons and in came silk and satin quilts, often thickly wadded to give a soft appearance (figs 74 and 75).

Designs were limited and rather formal, with relatively few pattern elements compared to earlier North Country quilts. But the quality of materials used gave a luxurious feel to the quilts and other items – dressing gowns, cushions and tea cosies – which were the stock in trade of these Workrooms. Prices reflected this move up-market with £9 being paid for a satin quilt in 1940, compared to an average £3 for a typical 'club quilt' of the same period.

Orders came from a wide area as the Workrooms' products became known and each of the items made had an embroidered tape – a 'Cash's tape' – sewn in to identify its origin. Amongst the orders completed were quilts for the then Queen (now the Queen Mother) and her daughters, Princess Elizabeth (Her Majesty the Queen) and H.R.H. Princess Margaret which were proudly put on show in the Barnard Castle Workroom in March 1938.

The scheme and the Workrooms are remembered with great affection and pride by those who worked there. They would undoubtedly have continued but war intervened and, with it, came a shortage of materials and a redirection of work strategy towards the war effort. This period of NIW activity remains the only time that making North Country quilts on a commercial basis was anything other than a home-based activity.

Fig 62 *Framed Centre Medallion Quilt*
Made by the Quilting Circle, Castleside, Co. Durham
c. 1920
Printed cottons
Bordered quilting design using border and filler patterns, including Squares, overlapping Chains, Wave, Old Joe's Chain, Rose and Wave, and Wavy Line
198 cm x 234 cm (78 x 92 inches)
Private collection

Fig 63 *Wholecloth wedding quilt*

Made by M. Elizabeth Shepherd of Amble, Northumberland, for her son (who never married)

1935

Cotton sateen, pink and yellow

Bordered quilting design with Rose and Plait motifs; Shell border (with corners from a bentwood chair seat pattern); Square Diamond and Square fillers

214 cm x 254 cm (84 x 100 inches)

Collection: Beamish: The North of England Open Air Museum, Co. Durham

Fig 64 *Wholecloth quilt* (detail)

Made by Elizabeth Featherstone (née Peart) of Haltwhistle, Northumberland (originally of Gold Hill, Weardale)

c. 1920

Flowered cotton top, reverse white cotton Strip quilting design with lined Cable border pattern; Diamond filler

226 cm x 249 cm (89 x 98 inches)

Private collection

Fig 65 *Wholecloth quilt*
Made by Hannah Petty of Nenthead, Cumberland (see fig 57)
c. 1920
Flowered cotton top, spotted red cotton reverse, piped edges
Strip quilting design with Bellows border pattern; Diamond filler
223 cm x 233 cm (88 x 92 inches)
Private collection

Fig 66 *Wholecloth quilt*
Maker unknown, provenance probably Northumberland
c. 1920-1930
Cotton sateen, pink and 'old gold'
Bordered quilting design marked by a quilt designer with Rose, Flat Iron, Leaf and Shell; Hammock with Rose borders; Square Diamond filler
210 cm x 243 cm (82.5 x 95.5 inches)
Collection: The Bowes Museum, Barnard Castle, Co. Durham

Fig 67 *Wholecloth quilt* (detail)

Designed quilt top, quilted and finished by Lilian Hedley of Chester-le-Street, Co. Durham

Designed 1924-1926; quilted 1988

'Old gold' cotton sateen

Bordered quilting design marked by a quilt designer with Sunflower, Flat Iron, Sycamore Leaf, Shell and Leaf motifs; freehand motifs; Square Diamond filler

218 cm x 228 cm (86 x 90 inches)

Collection: Shipley Art Gallery, Gateshead (Tyne & Wear Museums)

Fig 68 *Strippy quilt* (detail)

Made by Nancy Lister of Castleside, Co. Durham, with her aunt; design drawn by Mrs Gowland of Wolsington, Weardale

c. 1925

Pink and 'old gold' cotton sateen

Strip quilting design with lined Running Feather border pattern; Diamond filler

196 cm x 238 cm (77 x 90 inches)

Private collection

NORTH COUNTRY QUILTS: LEGEND AND LIVING TRADITION

Fig 69 *Framed Star quilt - Sanderson Star* (detail)
Maker unknown, top designed and pieced by a quilt designer
c. 1910-1920
Cotton sateen
Bordered quilting design following piecing with Rose in a Ring centre and freehand patterns; Cable Twist and freehand feathered borders; outer border of Weardale Chain
224 cm x 234 cm (88 x 92 inches)
Collection: Beamish: The North of England Open Air Museum, Co. Durham

Fig 70 *Framed Star quilt - Sanderson Star*
Designed and made by Elizabeth Sanderson of Allenheads, Northumberland
c. 1910-1920
Turkey red and white cotton
Bordered quilting design following piecing with Rose in a Ring centre and freehand patterns; Cable Twist and freehand feathered borders; outer border of Plait pattern
221 cm x 232 cm (87 x 91 inches)
Private collection

Fig 71 *Pieced Strippy quilt - Streak o' Lightning* (detail)

Maker: community in Carr Shield, Allendale, Northumberland

c. 1930

Printed and white cottons, white cotton reverse marked with quilting design in blue pencil

Bordered quilting design, said to have been marked by Elizabeth Sanderson, with feathers, leaves and scalloped Wavy Line border with Rose and Flower Spray motifs (includes innovative motif patterns)

222 cm x 254 cm (87.5 x 100 inches)

Private collection

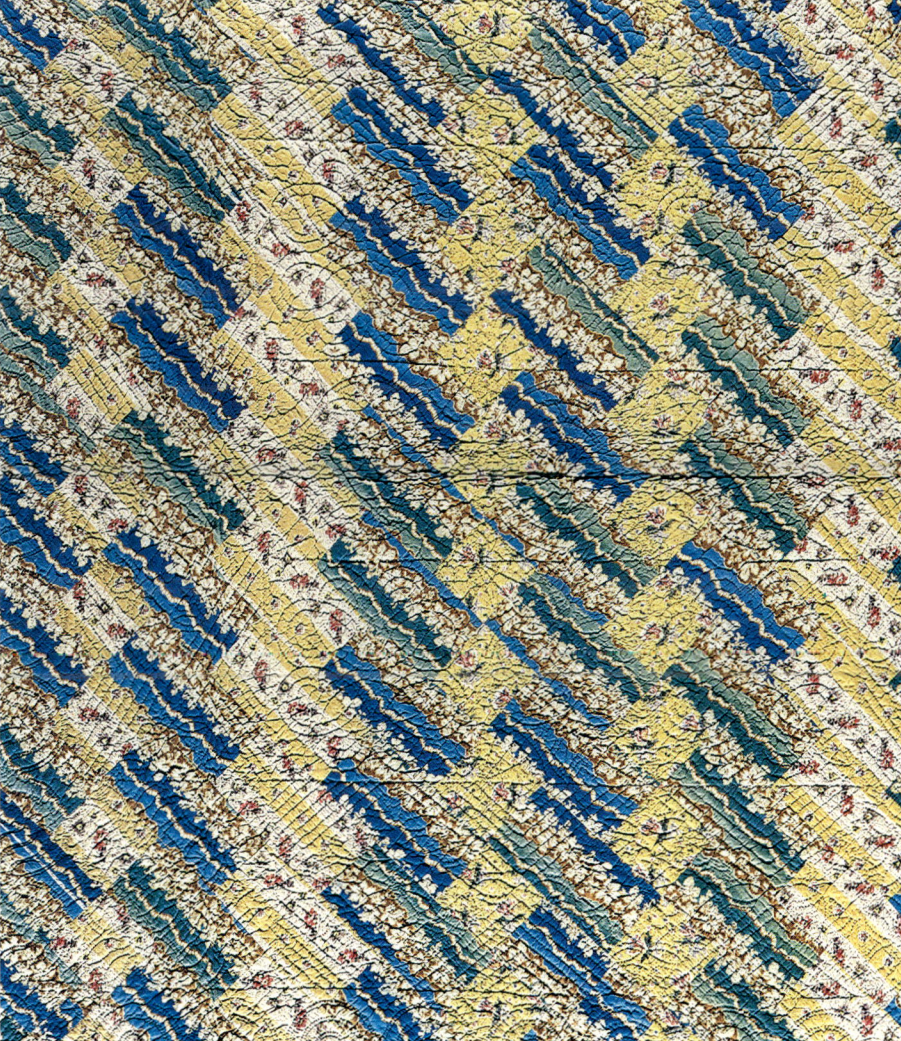

Fig 72 *Pieced quilt* (detail)

Maker: community in Carr Shield, Allendale, Northumberland

c. 1930

Printed cottons, some 1830s-1840s dress fabrics, cream cotton reverse marked with quilting design in blue pencil

Bordered quilting design, said to have been marked by Elizabeth Sanderson, with centre of concentric Circles, Lovers' Knot and filled Bellows motifs; Geometric and double-lined Wavy Line borders; innovative corner motifs

223 cm x 226 cm (88 x 89 inches)

Private collection

Fig 73 *Wholecloth quilt*
Made by Mary Ann Renwick of Carr Shield, Allendale, Northumberland
c. 1930
Cotton sateen top, reverse white cotton
Bordered quilting design, said to have been marked by Elizabeth Sanderson, with Large Rose centre; Feather Wreath and Rose motifs; lined Feather, Bellows and Wavy Line borders
242 cm x 245 cm (95 x 96.5 inches)
Private collection

POST WAR CHANGES AND NEW PATRONAGE

Fig 75 *Wholecloth quilt* (below)
Made by the Northern Industries Workrooms, Barnard Castle, Co. Durham
c. 1935-1936
Yellow silk satin
Bordered quilting design with Bellows and Star centre; Rose borders
102 cm x 167 cm (40 x 66 inches)
Collection: The Bowes Museum, Barnard Castle, Co. Durham

Fig 74 *Wholecloth quilt* (above)
Made by the Northern Industries Workrooms, Barnard Castle, Co. Durham
c. 1934
Pink silk satin top, cream tussore silk back
Bordered quilting design with Rose in a Ring, Straight Feather and Corn Sheaf motifs; Straight Feather borders; and Square Diamond filler
150 cm x 188 cm (59 x 74 inches)
Collection: The Bowes Museum, Barnard Castle, Co. Durham

Fig 76 *Bed jacket*
Made by Nancy Alderson (later Mrs Brass) of Barnard Castle in the Northern Industries Workrooms, Barnard Castle, Co. Durham
1933-1940
Cream silk satin, lined with cream silk
Quilted with Scalloped border, Square Diamond filler and Clamshell on the collar
Collection: The Bowes Museum, Barnard Castle, Co. Durham

Fig 77 *Wholecloth cot quilt*
Maker unknown, provenance probably Co. Durham
c. 1930-1932, included in WI exhibition at The Bowes Museum, 1930s
Silk, cream and pale blue
Bordered quilting design with Rose in a Ring, Straight Feather, Corn Sheaf and Fan motifs; Feather Twist with Rose in a Ring borders; and Square Diamond filler
91.5 cm x 132 cm (36 x 52 inches)
Collection: The Bowes Museum, Barnard Castle, Co. Durham

1939~1970
Bright Stars in an Age of Decline

The years that followed the Second World War were a low point for North Country quilting and, were it not for the efforts of a handful of individuals and the Women's Institute, the craft might have died out altogether. The reasons were both practical and social. Fabrics were initially in short supply after rationing during the war years. Changes in taste influenced both the choice and availability of fabrics; shiny rayons, taffetas and satins (made from man-made fibres) together with Shantung silk and crêpe de chine were in vogue for bedroom furnishings. The North Country quilts of this era, all Wholecloth quilts by now, reflected this changing fashion and it must be said that this choice of fabrics, particularly the man-made fibre fabrics, finds less favour amongst quilters and quilt enthusiasts today.

But perhaps social factors – changing attitudes and changing lifestyles for women – were of even greater influence. Hand-stitched quilts had come to be regarded as old-fashioned, elements of a previous era's domesticity that was consigned to history. Moreover, few women in the North of England now knew how to quilt; quilting had ceased to be a common practice so skills were rarely passed on and, in most households, that essential tool – the quilting frame – had been discarded. Even mat-making, if anything an even more entrenched domestic activity than quilting, virtually ceased in these post-war years. And those who had watched their mothers or grandmothers running quilt 'clubs' in mining communities wanted none of the drudge of such a hard-earned living.

As well as attitudes, women's lifestyles had changed. Continuing the pattern of the pre-war years, women increasingly worked outside the home leaving less time for activities such as quiltmaking. But there was no desire for hand-stitched quilts – that was the real root of decline. It was the era of 'modernity' and most women wanted their homes to be a reflection of the tastes purveyed in women's and lifestyle magazines of the time. If this was to include quilting, then it would be in some fashionable form such as the 'Italian' quilted cushions illustrated in the 'how to' pages of such magazines. On the bed would be a plump eiderdown, later a candlewick bedspread and later still a duvet.

As in the immediate pre-war age, North Country quilt-making was now confined to North East England alone – Northumberland and, especially, County Durham. Though for several generations a strong tradition in this region, in these post Second World War years it lost its cultural and community value. Was this simply because it was a women's tradition?

This bleak picture was, however, brightened by some isolated 'stars'. A handful of individuals continued to make quilts because it gave them personal pleasure and because they wanted to keep the practice of quiltmaking alive. Most had learnt from their mothers or grandmothers carrying on the direct vernacular tradition of the craft; the era of the 'book learning' quilter had yet to arrive. Three ladies emerged from amongst this small group, Mary Lough, Florence Fletcher and Amy Emms (see Focus page overleaf and p. 69), who all had the one talent that was otherwise lacking – a good eye for quilting design.

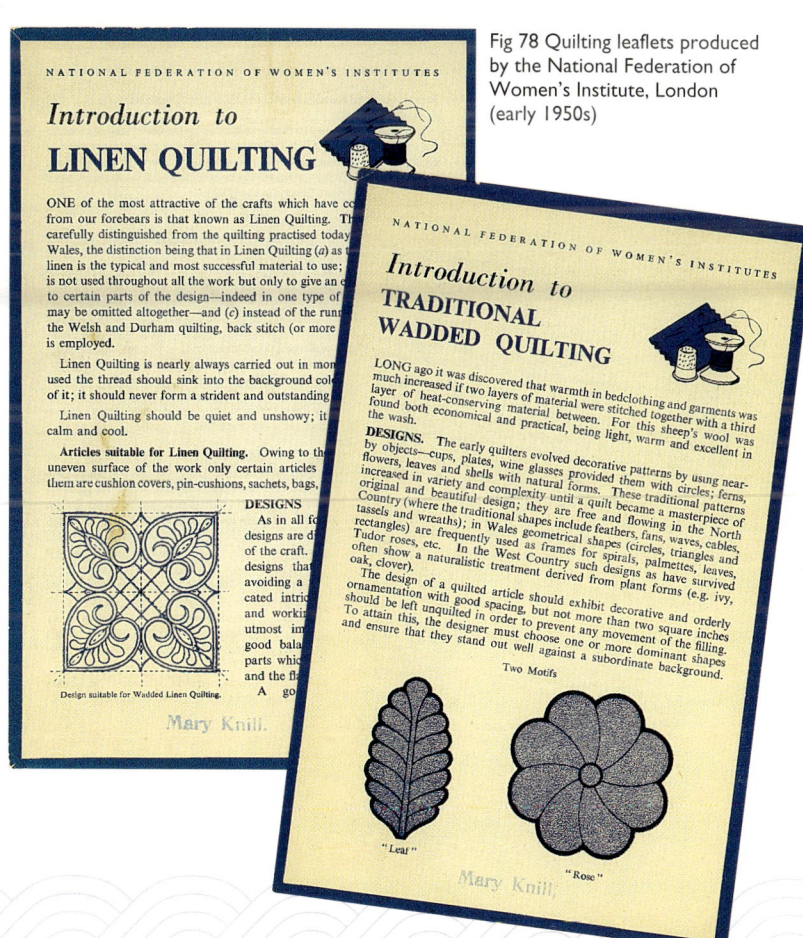

Fig 78 Quilting leaflets produced by the National Federation of Women's Institute, London (early 1950s)

Because North Country quiltmaking now solely concentrated on making Wholecloth quilts, the overall design of quilting patterns and design layout were of paramount importance in producing a quality quilt. Sadly, though, quilting design on Wholecloth quilts had gradually declined throughout the twentieth century. Perhaps less time for quilting had encouraged 'looser' designs that could be stitched more quickly; for those quilting for a living, such as miners' widows, more open designs with fewer patterns meant a saving of days or even weeks of stitching. By the 1950s, quilting design was generally poor with a limited pattern stock and little imagination or skill in co-ordinating patterns together.

Fig 79 Leaflet on 'Durham Quilting' produced by Durham County Federation of Women's Institutes

It was, in part, the influences of Mary Lough, Florence Fletcher and Amy Emms, together with the Durham Federation of Women's Institutes, which changed this. These three quilters became teachers of what, by this time, was universally called 'Durham quilting'. Mary Lough was the first, beginning her classes during the Second World War.

Responding to the pressures of teaching and also to open competitions which were now being held in certain areas, they all became more inventive and skilled in design. Yet, despite their evident abilities – as designers, quilters and, presumably, teachers over a considerable period of time – pupils rarely emerged to move the craft on to another generation and to a new level. Quilting was still regarded as a low-key, old-fashioned activity with little appeal to the dynamic, modern woman.

Even the efforts of the Women's Institute could not dispel this image, despite the success of their pre-war ventures, though they did help to keep the craft alive. Perceiving their responsibility to a local women's craft tradition, the Durham Federation Handicrafts Committee produced sets of 'Durham' quilting patterns, a 'how-to' booklet[1] and encouraged competition in shows. At the national level, the WI also introduced leaflets on quilting (fig 78).

Another remnant of pre-war quilting also managed to survive through the war years and beyond. One known quilt designer, Jennie Peart of Allendale, who had been apprenticed to Elizabeth Sanderson in the early years of the twentieth century, continued to mark out quilts for customers, together with her own apprentice Mary Fairless. There may have been others, no longer remembered, in Weardale. Their customers were not only individual quilters but, more especially, the church and chapel sewing clubs that still continued through into the 1950s and, occasionally, beyond. Though the desire to own a quilt might have diminished, social contact through quilting remained, for these clubs still fulfilled a community need in the pre-television years.

One signal of what was to come, however, was the exhibition of antique quilts held at The Bowes Museum in 1963. For the first time, North Country quilts from previous generations were on display in a gallery setting – an early sign of the resurgence of interest that was to explode in the last quarter of the twentieth century.

FOCUS:
MARY LOUGH AND FLORENCE FLETCHER OF WEARDALE

Born in 1886, Mary Lough absorbed the designs and techniques of quiltmaking from an early age, threading needles for her mother by candlelight. But though she learnt to quilt at a young age, it was not until later years that most of her quilts were made. First she became a teacher then raised her family, whilst living much of her life on the family farm in Witton-le-Wear. She was the first North Country quilter formally to teach quilting, taking advantage of the new drive for adult education by setting up classes in Weardale and beyond. By the 1950s, she had achieved a national reputation for her work, through exhibitions and quilting for high class customers. She died in 1968, aged 82. Her granddaughter remembers:

Fig 81 Mary Lough at work in her home at Witton-le-Wear

Fig 80 Mary Lough at the quilting frame in the early 1960s

In the early 1950s it was this energetic and thoughtful lady who paved the way for Mavis FitzRandolph to research and formally document North Country quilting in the pages of her timely book *Traditional Quilting*.[3] It was Florence Fletcher who 'opened doors' in the close-knit dales' communities for the incoming 'southerner'. Without her, it is doubtful whether FitzRandolph would have been able to document so fully the oral knowledge of past quilters, quilt designers and quiltmaking techniques still within dales' memory at that time. Later these two ladies collaborated on an instructional booklet;[4] highly popular, it ran to over four editions.

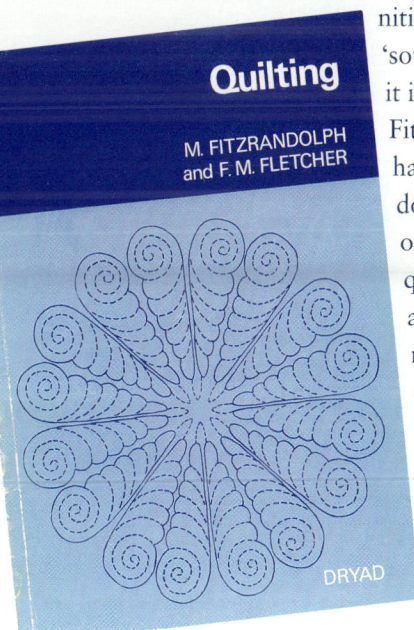

Fig 82 A practical guide to quilting by Mavis FitzRandolph and Florence Fletcher published by Dryad Press of Leicester

My grandmother exhibited her work in the Victoria and Albert Museum London and for a gorgeous dressing gown made for my sister she was awarded 100 marks ... this and other articles have appeared in needlework magazines ... [she] did quilting for the WI college Denman ... She could make a quilt for a double bed from start to finish in six weeks.[2]

Florence Fletcher, born in the early years of the twentieth century, was also a teacher but she then married a mining engineer and moved to Weardale. Already a skilled needlewoman whose grandmother had run a quilt 'club' in Ferryhill, she was captivated by the quality of the quilts she saw in Weardale and resolved to learn the craft. So she joined Mary Lough's classes and became a skilled quilter herself.

Sadly, early widowhood cut short Florence Fletcher's quilting activities and necessitated a return to teaching. Only after retirement in the mid-1960s was she able to go back to quilting and to once again passing on her skills.

Fig 83 *Wholecloth wedding quilt* (detail)

Made by Mary Lough, Witton-le-Wear, Co. Durham, for her granddaughter Beryl

c. 1956

Taffeta, with frilled and quilted valances

Bordered quilting design with Feather Wreath and Rose motifs; Cable Twist border; Square Diamond filler

247 cm x 261 cm (97 x 102.5 inches)

Private collection

Fig 84 *Wholecloth quilt* (detail)

Made by Mary Lough, Witton-le-Wear, Co. Durham

c. 1950s

Silk crêpe de chine

Bordered quilting design with centre of Cowslip leaves inside a large Feather Wreath, Scissors and Rose motifs; Feather Wreath and Rose borders; Square Diamond filler

223 cm x 224 cm (88 x 88.5 inches)

Collection: Beamish: The North of England Open Air Museum, Co. Durham

Fig 85 *Wholecloth quilt*

Made by Mary Lough, Witton-le-Wear, Co. Durham

c. 1950s

Cotton sateen, pink and 'old gold'

Bordered quilting design with Rose, Feather Wreath and Running Feather patterns

214 cm x 257 cm (86 x 101 inches)

Private collection

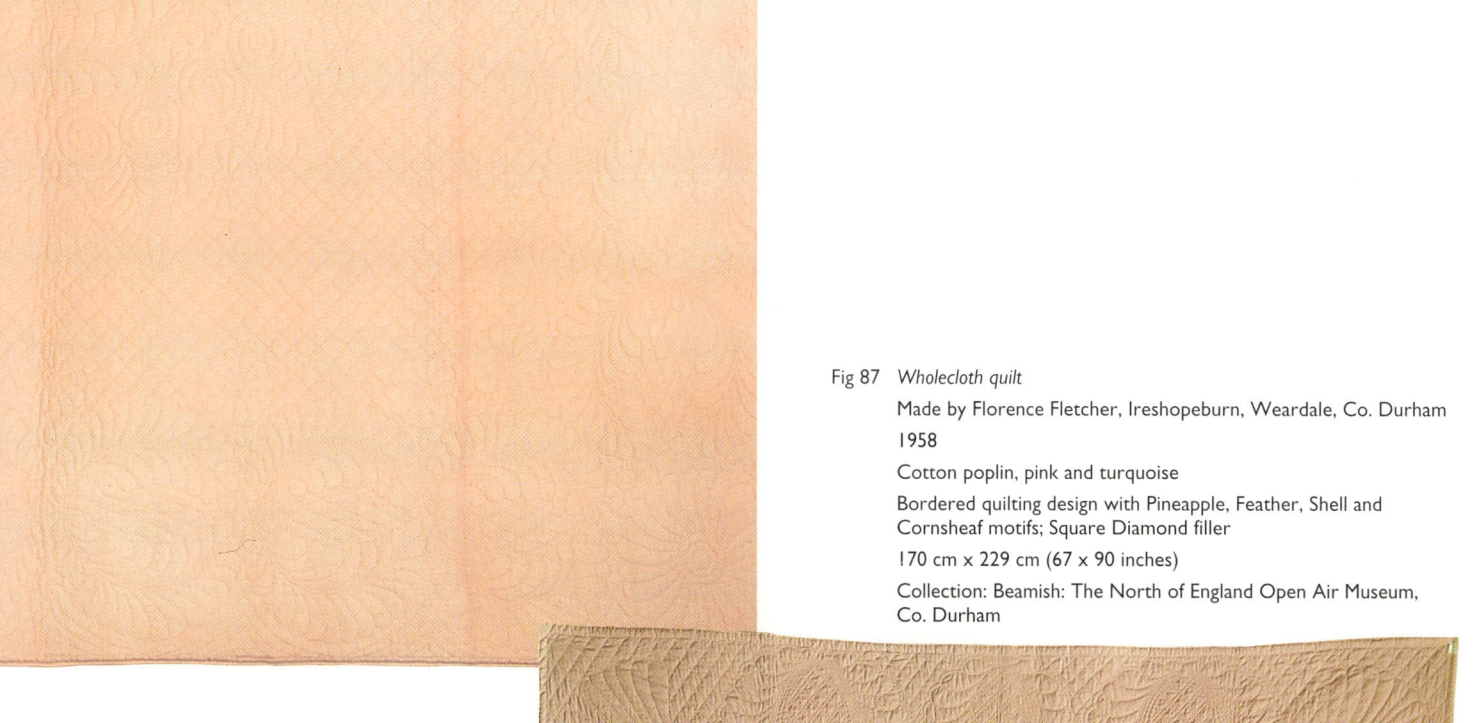

Fig 87 *Wholecloth quilt*
Made by Florence Fletcher, Ireshopeburn, Weardale, Co. Durham
1958
Cotton poplin, pink and turquoise
Bordered quilting design with Pineapple, Feather, Shell and Cornsheaf motifs; Square Diamond filler
170 cm x 229 cm (67 x 90 inches)
Collection: Beamish: The North of England Open Air Museum, Co. Durham

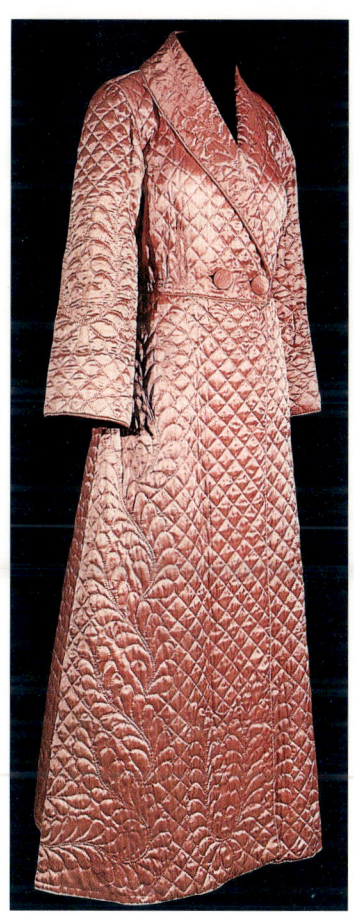

Fig 86 *Dressing gown*
Made by Nancy Peart of Wolsingham, Weardale, a pupil of Mary Lough
1948-49
Rayon satin
Quilted with Feather Wreath motifs; Feather Twist borders; Square Diamond filler
Collection: The Bowes Museum, Barnard Castle, Co. Durham

Fig 88 *Wholecloth quilt* (detail)
Maker unknown, design marked by a quilt designer, Weardale
c. 1950s
Cotton sateen, pink and yellow
Bordered quilting design with Rose, Flat Iron, Leaf and Filled Leaf motifs; Shell border; Square Diamond filler
203 cm x 239 cm (80 x 94 inches)
Private collection

Fig 89 *Wedding dress*
Made by Amy Emms, Sunderland, Co. Durham, for her daughter Olive
1957
Satin
Quilted with Feather and Cornsheaf motifs and Square Diamond filler patterns
Private collection

1970~2000
REVIVAL AND THE RISE OF THE ART QUILT

In retrospect, the final three decades of the twentieth century can be seen to have been a defining period for quilting (in the broad sense). It has changed, from a domestic craft producing functional furnishings for the home, to an art form practised by trained, professional artists who create art quilts to be seen in galleries and commercial venues as well as in private collections. The last twenty-five years have also seen quilting become a global business. Enthusiasts in every part of the developed world are now able to avail themselves of a wealth of fabrics, tools and books produced by an ever-increasing business fraternity. New groups and guilds, and the increasing number of quilt shows and events, provide opportunity to meet up with like-minded individuals all around the world.

How did these changes come about and what effect have they had on North Country quilting? The seeds of change from functional craft to art form were sown in the early 1970s with an exhibition called *Abstract Design in American Quilts*, first shown in 1971 at the Whitney Museum of American Art in New York. It later toured Europe (including Britain) and Japan. Curated by Jonathan Holstein and Gail van der Hoof from their own quilt collection, it placed antique American quilts in an art gallery setting provoking an assessment of their position as American art and, in Europe and Japan in particular, bringing American quilts to the attention of a new audience.

At the same time, the rise of feminism led to women exploring and questioning their past and current identities. Emerging from art schools, some sought to use fabric as a means of expression and, within quiltmaking, they recognized a gender connection with a past tradition that had produced works of strong aesthetic integrity. At first exploring traditional quiltmaking forms and practice, this new breed of quilt artist went on to challenge boundaries of form, function and technique, or to make provocative and political statements though the medium of the quilt.

Despite an ambivalence towards traditional forms of quiltmaking and its latent conservatism, an admiration for both North Country and Welsh quilts – the two most distinctive regional traditions of Britain – remained with some British quilt artists. Recognizing the sculptural and textural qualities imparted by heavy hand stitching and the graphic character of forms such as the Wholecloth and Strippy quilt, they have sought to draw out these qualities in selected works and to reinvest tradition, specifically the North Country one, with contemporary and challenging inferences (figs 101-111). These quilts bear witness to how wit, imagination, social and environmental consciousness, and political statement can all be etched into a vernacular form by re-working graphic layout, pattern form and the materials themselves in very personal ways. Michele Walker's *Assault and Battery* series, featuring the classic North Country feather motif in the most powerfully dramatic and emotive way, is emblematic of this (fig 102).

At the more popular level, the British 'quilt revival' was, and still is, largely influenced from North America. This revival began when visits and extended stays to the US and Canada brought women into contact with the American tradition of quilting. Fired with enthusiasm, they returned home to pass on their new found interest and skills. Magazine articles, books, exhibitions and television programmes followed, reaching an ever widening audience.

By 1979 there were sufficient enthusiasts, teachers and practitioners to form a guild – now The Quilters' Guild of the British Isles. Exhibitions, competitive shows, new quilting magazines and locally formed groups led to increasing numbers of active quilters in all parts of Britain which, in turn, led to a demand for classes and information sources. The explosion of interest in quilting over the past twenty years has been dramatic. Contributing factors include increased affluence and mobility, increased perceived freedom for women, the social opportunities afforded by quilting at a time when other women's organizations have declined, and the decline in dressmaking as clothes became relatively inexpensive. Quilting is now seen as a dynamic area of textile practice with a broad appeal to women who like to manipulate colour and fabric and enjoy the tactile experience of stitching.

The North of England has not been immune to this trend but it has taken time for this new breed of enthusiast quilter, schooled initially in the techniques of piecing and appliqué for American Block quilts, to look to the indigenous North Country tradition. Tools and techniques for speed cutting and piecing using sewing machines and rotary cutters offer quick ways to colourful Block quilts. With an emphasis on intricate quilting, the techniques of North Country quilts seem more difficult and more time intensive.

Quilting can indeed take time to master, even for those skilled in needlecrafts; design for Wholecloth quilting, in particular, is a demanding skill needing time to plan, and time and care to mark out designs on to fabric. Moreover, much of the appeal of the North Country quilt comes from the gently puckered lines of hand-worked running stitches which subtly outline patterns without sharply delineating them. Although machine quilting has an important and deserved place in contemporary quiltmaking, the character of the running stitch cannot be suitably replicated with a sewing machine. So making a traditional North Country quilt, now generally perceived as a Wholecloth quilt or perhaps a Strippy quilt, is rightly seen as a big investment in time and effort.

But with North Country quilting still (only just) alive through the work of Amy Emms and one or two others, both institutions and practitioners in the North East of England have been able to help local quilters break through these perceived barriers. Museums like The Bowes Museum in Barnard Castle and Beamish North of England Open Air Museum in Stanley, both in County Durham, continue to add to their quilt collections and to make quilts available for exhibitions, publications, workshops and special events. The Bowes Museum has regularly staged its own exhibitions, drawing on its fine collection. For ten years, the Museum has also been host to a series of Workers' Educational Association (WEA) quilting classes, taught by Elsie Walton of Weardale, herself a pupil of Amy Emms.

The role of the Shipley Art Gallery in Gateshead has also been pivotal. Building on an oral history tape archive programme established in 1979, which included research into quilting memories, the gallery initiated a series of biennial quilt exhibitions and an on-going teaching programme.

The exhibition series began in 1985 by showing the work of local 'grassroots' quilters and continued with this emphasis through the 1980s and early 1990s. The quilts shown were many and varied and, as the years progressed, included an increasing number of quilts which drew upon the North Country tradition.

Later, as the quilting audience matured in its taste, the gallery shifted to staging exhibitions incorporating more contemporary work, helping to promote the work of Britain's growing number of quilt artists. Its role in this has been of national importance. If the gallery's focus is no longer primarily on North Country quilting, its established reputation for quality art quilt exhibitions spotlights the region and emphasizes its current influential position.

The teaching programme was, initially, equally successful and included classes on North Country quilting from the early 1980s onwards. The first tutor was Amy Emms who already enjoyed a national reputation. My own series of classes followed but as gallery priorities and resources changed, the teaching programme ceased in the early 1990s. The seeds sown, however, were already bearing fruit and classes transferred to other venues with new, regionally-based teachers, such as Lilian Hedley, coming to the fore.

As skill and confidence have increased amongst local grassroots quilters, the appeal of making North Country quilts has grown, not least because of the opportunity it presents to revive a local tradition and to reinforce a sense of regional identity – still strong in the North of England. Concentrating chiefly on Wholecloth quilts, a group of accomplished local quilters has emerged whose fine quilts (figs 93-100) can be shown with pride alongside those of previous generations. Though recognizably within a traditional framework, there is a vibrancy and individuality to each piece which defies the criticism of retro-ism and conservatism with which traditions are so often charged.

And that is the challenge for North Country quilting – to take a revived practice forward, to recognize its basic strengths and qualities, and to continue to reinvigorate them as a living tradition.

Focus:
Amy Emms MBE of Sunderland and Weardale

Amy Emms was to become a quilting legend in her lifetime. She was born in Sunderland in 1904 to a mother already widowed who, like many women in the North East at that time in such circumstances, ran a quilting 'club'. So, for the young Amy, quilting was an everyday activity. At seven she began threading needles; by fourteen she was helping her mother make quilts. After leaving school, Amy followed the conventional route of office job and then marriage – at the age of 20 to Albert Emms, a stained-glass maker. Equally conventionally, they set up home with her mother, so joint quiltmaking continued despite motherhood and the onset of World War Two.

Fig 90 "One of my proudest moments" - Amy and Olive Emms in 1957 with Olive in the exquisite wedding dress (fig 89) made by her mother

Ever energetic and outward looking, Amy joined the British Legion. Soon she was leading a quilting group. Annual exhibitions in Sunderland followed, then evening class teaching in the 1950s. In 1967 Albert and Amy retired to St John's Chapel in Weardale but she was widowed soon afterwards. Seeking solace in her craft, she was encouraged to teach and to exhibit by the Women's Institute and the newly-established Beamish Museum. So when the revival of quilting in Britain began in the 1970s, it was not long before Amy came to the fore. The quality of her designs and superlative workmanship brought world-wide acclaim.

But it was not only her quilts that were admired. Amy became a regular contributor to the letters' page of the Quilters' Guild magazine, her prose revealing the endearing personality that captivated audiences at the many quilt shows and exhibitions she attended. The letters, battered out on an old manual typewriter with the speed of the trained typist that she was, 'talked' to the quilting world in idiosyncratic, conversational style. They loved it and took her to their hearts.

Fig 91 Amy Emms at the quilting frame working on her favourite Feather Twist border (c. 1980)

Although by now in her seventies, Amy began teaching again at the Shipley Art Gallery in Gateshead where she encountered a new audience, eager for knowledge and skill, but also questioning traditional methods. Rising to the challenge, she embraced the new, book-learning approach and, at 86 years of age, wrote *Amy Emms Story of Durham Quilting*.[1] It fulfilled a long-held ambition. In 1984 she was awarded an MBE for her 'services to quilting'.

Amy never stopped making quilts and took her final bow to the quilting world in May of 1998. At the age of 94, she attended a show in Malvern, winning over her audience, as ever, with her humour, dignity, knowledge and skill. She died a month later. Her life had spanned almost the entire twentieth century but it also spanned the cultural shift of quilting from a vernacular, sometimes insular, craft to an acclaimed textile art.

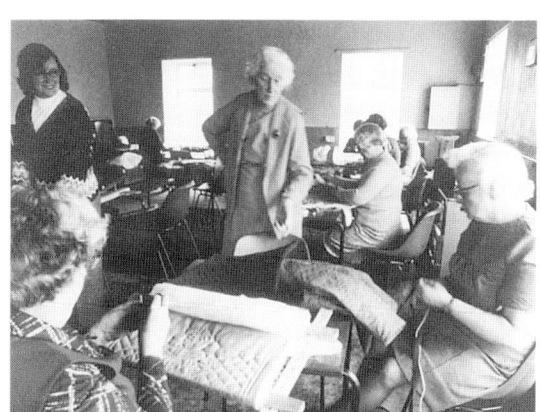

Fig 92 Amy Emms conducting a quilting class at Westgate-in-Weardale (mid 1970s)

REVIVAL AND THE RISE OF THE ART QUILT

Fig 94 *Unnamed Wholecloth quilt*
Amy Emms (1904-1998) of St John's Chapel, Weardale
Polyester satin, hand quilted (1997)
212 cm x 240 cm (83.5 x 94.5 inches)
Made by Amy Emms at the age of 93, this was the last quilt completed before her death in 1998
Private collection

Fig 93 *Unnamed Wholecloth quilt* (detail, opposite left)
Amy Emms (1904-1998) of St John's Chapel, Weardale
Cotton fabrics, hand quilted (1982)
109 cm x 147 cm (43 x 58 inches)
Commissioned by The Quilters' Guild for presentation to Deirdre Amsden after her term as the Guild's first President
Private collection

Fig 95 *Echoes of the Past*
Lilian Hedley of Chester-le-Street, Co. Durham
Cotton sateen, hand quilted (1988)
224 cm x 224 cm (88 x 88 inches)
Based on the design style of the Allendale/Weardale quilt designers, this elegant wholecloth quilt was a first prize winner for its maker at a national quilt show in 1988
Maker's collection

REVIVAL AND THE RISE OF THE ART QUILT

Fig 97 *Three Heads are Better than One*
Anne Tuck of Ponteland, Northumberland
Cotton fabrics, hand pieced and quilted (1990)
181 cm x 227 cm (71 x 89.5 inches)
An original interpretation of the pieced Strippy quilt, this bold design was commissioned for a book illustration
Maker's collection

Fig 96 *Springtime* (opposite left)
Emily Brown of Washington, Co. Durham
Cotton fabrics, hand quilted (1988-89)
206 cm x 226 cm (81 x 89 inches)
The first full double-bed sized quilt by the maker, it was designed and completed under the tutelage of Dorothy Osler and Lilian Hedley
Maker's collection

Fig 98 *French Curve Variation*
Maureen Avery of Newcastle upon Tyne
Cotton poplin, hand quilted (1989-90)
236 cm x 238 cm (93 x 93.5 inches)
Designed using a French Curve drawing template as the basic quilt motif, this original design was a first quilt from this maker
Maker's collection

Fig 99 *Lindisfarne Line*

Leila Anderson of Durham City

Cotton fabrics, hand quilted (1996)

226 cm x 239 cm (89 x 94 inches)

The design source for this intricately planned and exquisitely worked quilt is the famed Lindisfarne Gospels

Maker's collection

REVIVAL AND THE RISE OF THE ART QUILT

Fig 100 *Rose in a Ring*
Wendy Baxter of Ponteland, Northumberland
Cotton fabrics, hand quilted (1992-93)
89 cm x 119 cm (35 x 47 inches)
Adapted from a tutor's workshop design, this small wholecloth quilt is a complex of traditional patterns individually interpreted
Maker's collection

Fig 101 *Mediaeval Strippy* (detail)
C. June Barnes of Hastings, East Sussex
Silk fabrics, machine quilted (1999)
152 cm x 122 cm (60 x 48 inches)
Originally made for an exhibition of Red and White quilts, the original red fabric in this piece 'ran' so the maker dyed the finished quilt purple - with stunning effect
Private collection

Fig 102 *Assault and Battery 2*

Michele Walker of Brighton, East Sussex

Plastic and PVC materials, poultry feather filling, machine and hand appliqué, machine quilted (2000)

142 cm x 219 cm (56 x 86 inches)

The second in a series of quilts symbolizing the suffering imposed on poultry by factory farming methods; the Curled Feather image is a classic North Country motif and the bar code reflects the strippy quilt design

Maker's collection

Fig 103 *Retread 3*

Michele Walker of Brighton, East Sussex

Thermal (rubber coated) curtain lining, machine pieced, appliqué and machine quilted (1996)

200 cm x 200 cm (78 x 78 inches)

Inspired by traditional North Country wholecloth quilting but made as a response to the environmental devastation caused by the M3 extension through Twyford Down, Hampshire; the quilting pattern is based on a car tyre dump

Maker's collection

Fig 104 *Colourwash and Electric Stripes*

    Deirdre Amsden of London

    Cotton fabrics, machine pieced, hand quilted (1999)

    117 cm x 196 cm (46 x 77 inches)

    The use of shaded and dramatically contrasting colours bring energy and tension to this piece which is quilted in a Feather Twist border pattern in memory of Amy Emms who favoured this border on her wholecloth quilts

    Maker's collection

Fig 105 *Colourwash Spillikins*

    Deirdre Amsden of London

    Cotton fabrics, machine pieced, hand quilted (1998)

    161 cm x 205 cm (63.5 x 80.5 inches)

    Inspired by the childhood memory of a favourite game 'Pick-up-Sticks', the 'sticks' appear on a simulated Strippy quilt background quilted to resemble the wood grained floor in which the game was played

    Maker's collection

Fig 106 *Basket quilt*

    Lynn Setterington of Manchester

    Cotton fabrics, hand quilted with couched centre basket motif (1998)

    155 cm x 155 cm (61 x 61 inches)

    A contemporary re-working of the white wholecloth quilt using the basket symbol as a metaphor for fertility, happiness and plenty

    Maker's collection

Fig 107 *Unsung Heroes* (detail)

    Lynn Setterington of Manchester

    Cotton fabrics, hand quilted (1995)

    295 cm x 156 cm (116 x 61.5 inches)

    Based on reflections of an early Spring visit to the gardens at Belsay Hall, Northumberland, when the maker was artist-in-residence; the motifs reflect gardening activity and early Spring flowers but the overall style simulates a Strippy quilt

    Collection: Shipley Art Gallery, Gateshead (Tyne & Wear Museums)

NORTH COUNTRY QUILTS: LEGEND AND LIVING TRADITION

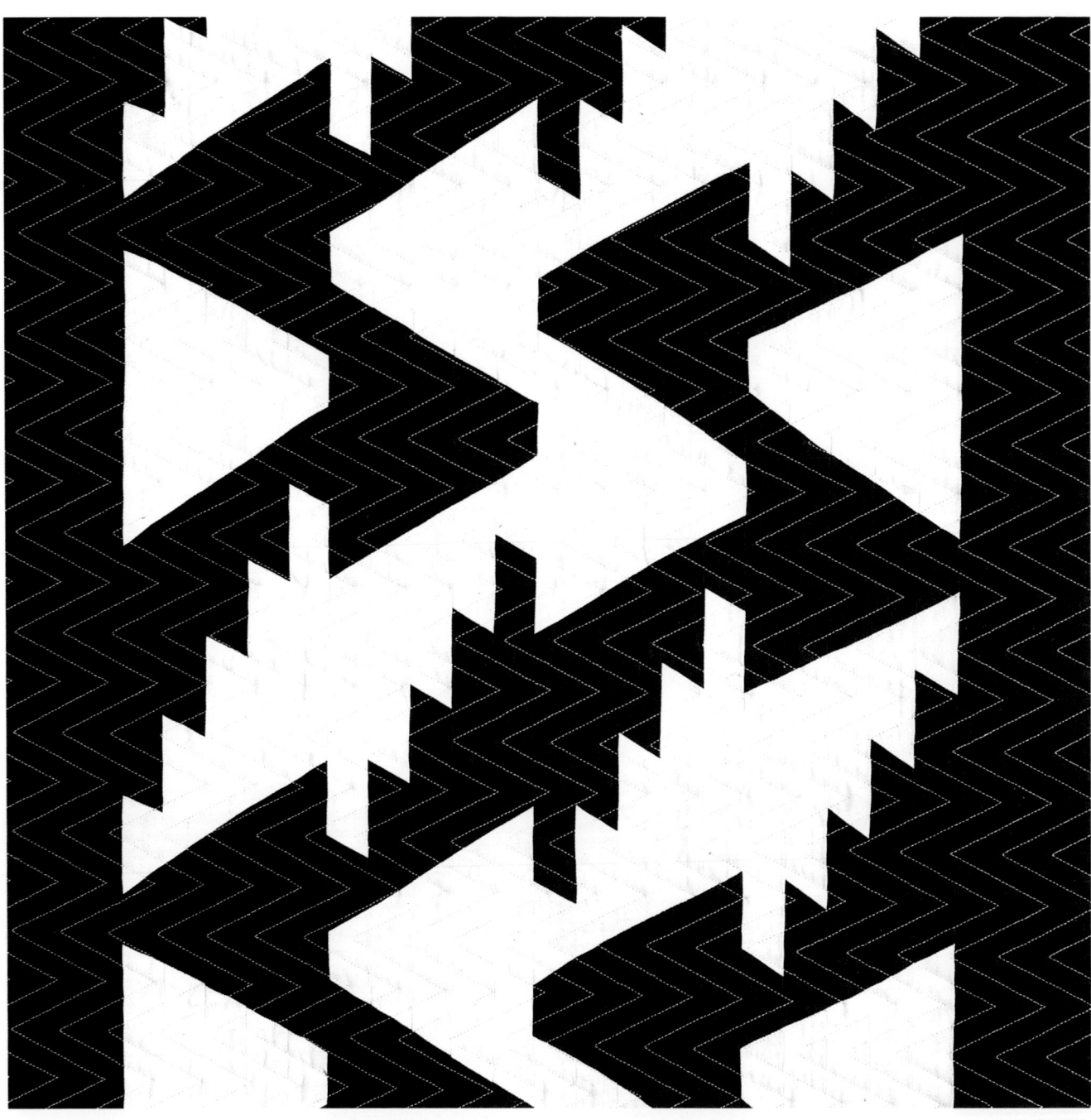

Fig 108 *Black and White Bars II*
Pauline Burbidge of Allanton, near Duns, Berwickshire
Cotton fabrics, machine pieced and machine quilted (1986)
137 cm x 162 cm (54 x 64 inches)
One of a series of hangings designed using simple, pieced, tessellated shapes and quilted using a multi-needle industrial machine
Maker's collection

REVIVAL AND THE RISE OF THE ART QUILT

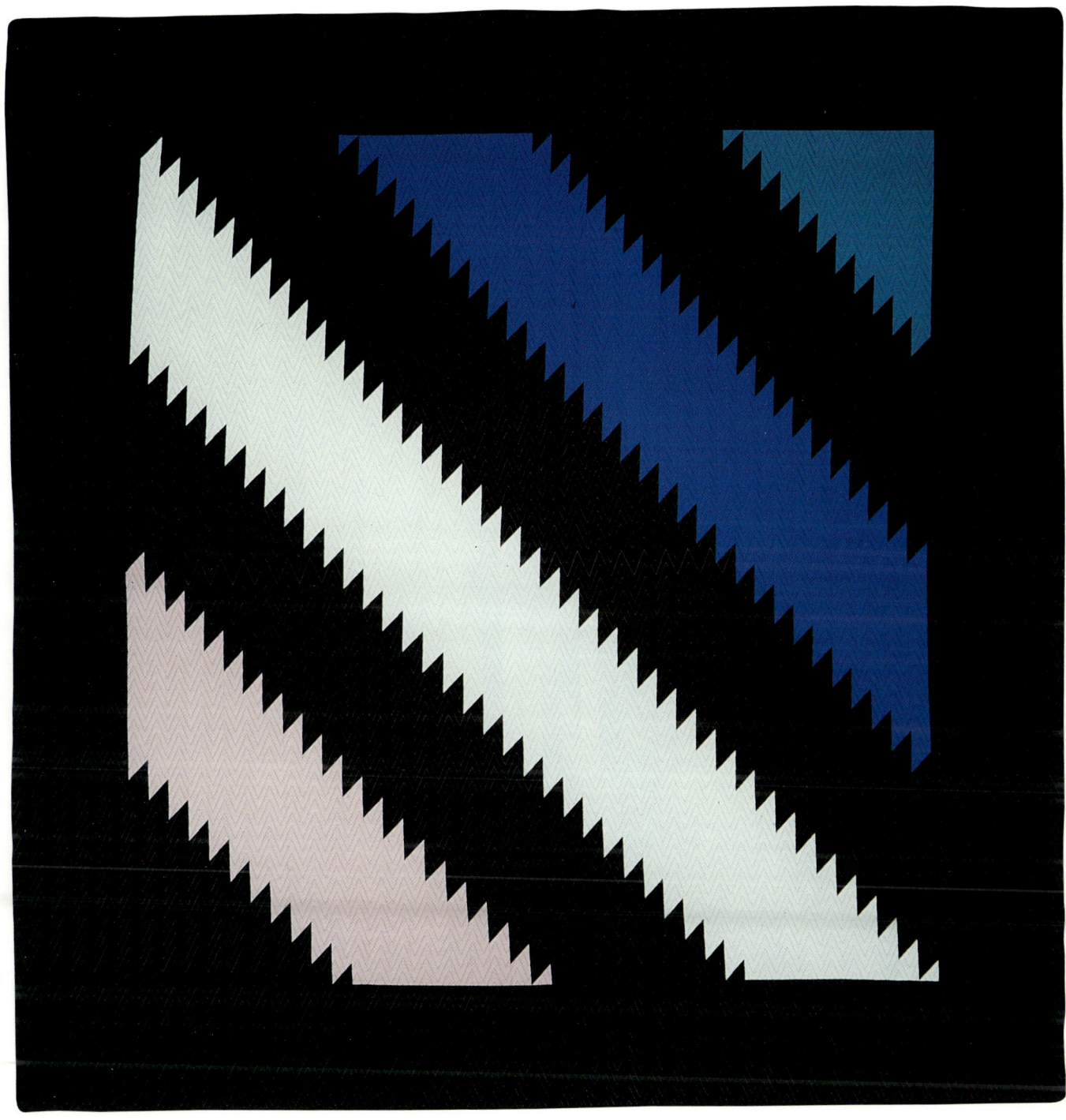

Fig 109 *Diagonal Zig-Zag*
Pauline Burbidge of Allanton, near Duns, Berwickshire
Cotton fabrics, machine pieced and machine quilted (1986)
208 cm x 208 cm (82 x 82 inches)
Designed with simple geometric shapes, this bed quilt was one of a short production run of practical quilts from this professional quilt artist and was quilted with a multi-needle industrial machine
Maker's collection

Fig 110 *The Farlam Angels*

    Margaret Bray (1930-1995) of Farlam, near Brampton, Cumbria

    Satin, hand quilted in white and brown thread (1993)

    149 cm x 218 cm (58.5 x 86 inches)

    Working within the bounds of the wholecloth quilt, this figurative work depicts the legendary 'angels' said to appear on the island in Talkin' Tarn, Cumbria, the scene of the tragic drowning of three children

    Private collection

Fig 111 *Shifting Sands XI*

    Helen Parrott of Sheffield

    Cotton calico, hand stitched in linen thread (1999)

    61 cm x 86 cm (24 x 34 inches)

    The works in this series seek to create a whole, a complete structure, using simple marks, minimal forms and ordinary materials

    Maker's collection

Appendix: Quilt Types, Quilting Designs and Quilting Techniques

This appendix section looks at the nature of North Country quilts and how they are made. It is not intended as a thorough guide to quiltmaking, but rather as a practical guide to an understanding of the structure of these quilts and to the terms used to categorize them.

The section also provides a 'library' of the most common quilting motifs used in North Country quilting from the early nineteenth century onwards. It is these patterns that gave North Country quilting its particular style and character, and so they are the main elements of regional distinctiveness which hallmark these quilts.

QUILT TYPES

Quilts are, in essence, a sandwich – a quilt top and quilt back with some form of wadding in between – with the layers stitched together by means of quilting. In terms of design, the quilt top may be one design, the quilt back may be a different design and the quilting itself may be of yet another design.

It is the nature of the quilt top which defines the quilt type. The quintessential North Country quilts are now considered to be Wholecloth and Strippy quilts but, in fact, many different kinds of Pieced (patchwork) and Appliquéd quilts were made in the northern counties of England from the Industrial Revolution onwards. Most fall into well-recognized quilt categories but others defy conventional description, for quilt makers are individuals, and inventive or quirky individuals will always produce something 'off the norm'.

Wholecloth quilts

The classic Wholecloth quilt is made from a single fabric, strips of which are seamed together to make up the quilt top. In recent years, full bed-width fabric has become available so removing this need for seaming. Before 1930, most North Country Wholecloth quilts were made from cotton or cotton sateen but 1930s' taste introduced glossy, luxury fabrics such as silk and satin (e.g. fig 77). This vogue carried through into the 1950s but declined thereafter.

The Wholecloth quilt has little inherent design in the quilt top itself; instead it presents a flat canvas to the quilter on which to show off her design abilities and technical prowess in the craft of quilting *per se*. One simple variation from the uniform canvas, however, is the Framed Wholecloth, popular in the early years of the twentieth century (fig 42).

Strippy quilts

The Strippy quilt is made from broad strips of fabric sewn together in a (usually) vertical 'set'. Most Strippy quilts are in the form of the Classic Strippy (e.g. fig 40) with two contrasting fabrics used for the strips, but two common variations are the Pieced Strippy (fig 45), and Broad and Narrow Strippy (fig 44).

Traditionally, cotton or cotton sateen were the fabrics of choice for Strippy quilts. Though all kinds of cottons, plain and printed, were used, combinations of a pastel tone with white were especially common before the 1920s. Simple to make and simple to plan, these were everyday quilts.

Pieced and Appliquéd Quilts

First, a few definitions. The craft of patchwork (or piecing as it is now often called) involves seaming fabric shapes together; appliqué, on the other hand, is the term used when fabric shapes are applied onto a fabric base. Both techniques are long established and can be worked in elaborate fashion in a variety of fabrics. In practice, most North Country style Pieced and Appliquéd quilts are of cotton fabrics, though Pieced wool quilts are not unknown.

The repertoire of North Country quilts includes a surprising variety of quilt types which include the techniques of piecing and appliqué. Many quilts include both techniques on the same quilt top, so they will be described together, broadly divided into two main categories - the Framed quilt and the Block quilt - based on the basic units of the quilt and how they fit together.

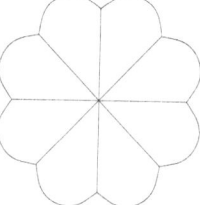

Rose 1

Rose 2

Rose in a Ring

Tulip

Sunflower

Four-petalled Flower

The Framed Quilt. This has a centre, around which a series of borders is sewn – at least four, and maybe several more (e.g. fig 12). The borders can be pieced, appliquéd or of single fabric; they may increase in width towards the outer edges of the quilt; and there is often an alternation of pieced or appliqué borders with borders of single fabric. Early Framed quilts also tend to be Scrap quilts, i.e. made from fabrics from the scrap bag rather than specially bought fabrics.

The nature of the centre of a Framed quilt can define it further. In the early 1800s, there was a vogue for using large printed chintz panels as quilt centres (e.g. fig 10). This led to the term Centre (or Central) Medallion quilts, now commonly applied to any Framed quilt with a basic centrepiece – a fabric panel, or a pieced or appliquéd centre (e.g. fig 13).

There are two common sub-types of North Country Framed quilt. The first is the Framed Diamond in the Square (e.g. fig 8) in which one square is set 'on point' with triangular sections attached to its sides to make a larger central square. This type of Framed quilt was equally common in the other regional quilting traditions of Britain. The second type is unique to North Country quilting. The Framed Star quilt – the generic name applied to a quilt type now more commonly known as the 'Sanderson Star' – was created by Elizabeth Sanderson of Allenheads and taught to her apprentices. Always in two contrasting colours, usually of cotton sateen, this striking design is instantly recognizable whenever, and wherever, a quilt of this type turns up (figs 69 and 70).

The Block Quilt. A series of pieced or appliquéd block units, usually square, make up this quilt type. Often considered uniquely American, it did indeed reach a peak of elaboration and invention in the New World in the nineteenth century. But block quilts, both pieced and appliquéd, were also made in the northern counties of England in a style which reflects the usual characteristics of North Country quilts – restricted colour palette, often just one colour with white; simple block form; and curvilinear quilting design (figs 17 and 34-36).

The block types may have remained simple and colour combinations restricted so that the North Country quiltmaker could continue to exercise her quilting skills, but she was clearly aware of the forms and sophistications of quilt 'setting', i.e. ways of combining quilt blocks together. So, in parallel with other quiltmaking traditions, blocks set 'on point' (fig 16) and block combinations which produce a graphic overall design (fig 17) can be found amongst recognizably North Country pieced and appliquéd quilts.

QUILTING DESIGNS

When the layers of a quilt are quilted together, the stitching has several functions. It holds the wadding securely in place; it produces a softly sculptured, three-dimensional surface; and it forms a decorative design which is an integral part of the quilt's visual and tactile appeal.

This decorative design – the quilting design – is made up of a selection of quilting patterns grouped together in a design plan or layout which is superimposed onto the quilt top. So, there are two separate elements to consider – quilting patterns and quilting layouts.

Quilting Patterns

Patterns are the basic units – the building blocks – that are co-ordinated together within a planned layout to make up the quilting design. The key to good quilting design is the way in which patterns are combined, together with the basic quality of line in the patterns themselves.

North Country quilting patterns can be broadly grouped into motifs, borders and fillers, according to the part they play in the quilting design as a whole:

1. Motif patterns are complete patterns with outlines that do not need to interlock. They can be used singly, as symmetrical repeats or in organized groups; most are drawn with a pattern template. More individual motif patterns are identified with the style of North Country quilting than other pattern types. The commonest ones are illustrated in this Appendix but numerous variations of many of these patterns (e.g. Rose, Feather Wreath) also exist.

2. Border patterns either frame the central area of a quilt (in a Bordered layout – see below) or are worked down the length of a quilt (in a Strip layout). There are three main forms of border pattern: geometrically divided borders (the oldest type); interlocking border patterns; and repeated motifs. Pattern templates are used to draft most borders. Common border patterns associated with particular time periods are illustrated in previous chapters.

Open Flower

Shell 1

Shell 2

Small Feather

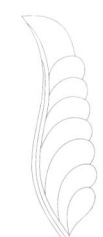
Goosewing

Curled Feather

3. Filler patterns fill the spaces between motifs and borders and, occasionally, within motifs and borders. On North Country quilts, five common filler patterns appear: Wave (fig 32); Clamshell (fig 16); Wine Glass or Plate (overlapping circles); Diamonds (fig 68); and by far the commonest, Square Diamonds (fig 67). The two latter patterns need only a line tool for drawing; the others use some form of template (wine glass or plate in the eponymous patterns) repeated over the surface to be filled.

On North Country quilts, patterns inevitably evolved over time. The early nineteenth century geometric borders and freeform naturalistic patterns evolved into bolder, stylized motifs and interlocking, curvilinear borders. This pattern evolution went hand in hand with the evolution in design which led to the characteristic, flowing designs of late nineteenth and twentieth century North Country quilts. Motifs and borders all developed a curved or scalloped outline; only the geometric filler patterns remained as straight line patterns.

Another general trend was a decrease in the number of individual patterns used within a quilt design; this is particularly marked in quilts from the post Second World War period. The variety of border and filler patterns used also decreased on twentieth century quilts when compared with those of the previous century.

Quilting Layouts

Most North Country quilts fall into one of three basic layouts – the Bordered layout, the Strip layout and the Allover layout – but numerous variations of these three basic forms also exist. Like quilt types, the knowledge of how to work these quilting layouts and how to fit patterns into them formed part of the core of oral knowledge passed between generations.

The Bordered Layout. In this design plan, individual quilting patterns are grouped into a centre design set in a central field with one or more borders around. Corner designs may or not be added. The central field is usually quilted with a filler pattern. On quilts made before the late nineteenth century, these sections of the quilt surface were often clearly defined by a double row of quilting lines, about ½ inch (1.3 cm) or ¾ inch (2 cm) apart (e.g. fig 20), but as the influence of the quilt designers spread, these defining lines were dropped though the sections clearly remained (compare figs 18 and 55).

Most North Country Wholecloth and Framed quilts are quilted with a Bordered layout. It is also the layout found on most Wholecloth quilts made throughout Britain over centuries past.

The Strip Layout. In this plan, the quilting patterns are arranged in rows running down the quilt (e.g. figs 46 and 48). Simpler than the Bordered layout, with no corners to turn, it was probably devised for quilting Strippy quilts but was also used on Wholecloth, Pieced and Appliquéd quilts. It is rare to find this quilting design on quilts other than North Country quilts.

The Allover Layout. A single pattern, usually a filler pattern, is used over the whole quilt surface in this layout. This type of quilting layout is often found on pieced or appliquéd quilts where a more complex quilting design would not show to advantage (figs 12 and 16).

Feather Wreath

Small leaf

Cowslip leaf

Flat-iron

Swirl and Cockscomb

Fan

MAKING A QUILT

Making a North Country quilt involves a series of technical stages which have changed but little over time. The contemporary grassroots quilter or art quilter will follow much the same process as both the pre- and post-Industrial Revolution quilters.

1. **Preparing the quilt top.** The fabric top of the quilt is first prepared according to design – Wholecloth, Strippy, Pieced and/or Appliquéd.

2. **Marking out the quilting design.** The quilting design is then drawn onto the fabric top using a suitable marker – pencil, coloured pencil, needle and chalk were, and are, all common marking tools. The precise choice of marker will depend on the type and colour of fabric. Templates for the individual patterns in the design are positioned on the fabric top and drawn around lightly; filling patterns are marked with measuring tools. (For Strippy quilts, this marking out stage was often deferred until the quilt was set in the frame – see stage 5).

3. **Preparing the backing and wadding.** The backing for the quilt also needs preparation – maybe as much as the quilt top. Many North Country quilts were made to be reversible with perhaps a Strippy back to a Wholecloth quilt. Traditionally, cotton wadding, bought in rolls, was opened up and allowed to 'rise'. Today a wide range of polyester waddings is available as well as all natural fibre forms – cotton, wool and silk.

4. **Layering.** This is the term used to describe assembling the fabric layers of the quilt and tacking them together. It is only strictly necessary when quilting in a hoop – the modern tool now often used instead of a large quilting frame.

5. **Setting in a frame.** Up to about 1980, quilts were quilted in a traditional-style frame – two long rails and two shorter, adjustable stretchers which rest on table tops, chests or trestles when in use. Lengths of webbing are attached to the rails. This basic frame is still used though more sophisticated free-standing frames are also on the market. The back of the quilt is first stitched to the webbing with the surplus rolled on to the far rail. Then the wadding and quilt top are placed in position and stitched to the near rail. With the layers in place, fabric strips are looped around the stretchers and pinned to the sides of the quilt to put it under light tension. This basic method has stood the test of time, though some quilters prefer to layer and tack a quilt together before setting it in a frame.

6. **Setting in a hoop.** After layering and tacking, the quilt is set into a quilting hoop (or small quilt frame); these can be bought in a variety of sizes. It is usual to begin quilting in the centre of the quilt and work outwards.

7. **Quilting.** The traditional stitch on North Country quilts is a running stitch worked by rocking the needle backwards and forwards and taking several stitches at a time. Threads used were coarse cotton or linen; later finer dressmaking threads were used on silk and satin quilts. Today a wide variety of threads is available both for hand and machine quilting.

8. **Finishing.** When quilting is complete, the quilt is removed from the frame or hoop and the raw edges finished. On North Country quilts, the traditional finish was to turn edges in, matching the two folds, and stitch them together with one or two rows of stitches. This is known as a butt or knife edge. On twentieth century quilts, these finishing rows were, more often than not, worked by machine until the 1950s when the vogue changed and hand finished edges, including piped edges, became once again the common finishing technique.

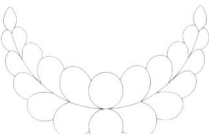

Penny Ha' penny

Weardale wheel

True Lovers' Knot

Scissors

Fleur-de-Lis

Four Hearts

Notes and References

Introduction

1. The Bowes Museum held quilt exhibitions in 1938 and 1946, then again in 1963 (curated by the then Folk Life Assistant, Anne Ward) and, more recently, the Costume and Textiles Curator Joanna Hashagen staged exhibitions in 1983, 1990, 1991 and 1997.

2. A 'true quilt' has a top fabric, a backing fabric and a layer of filling (wadding or batting) in between with the layers stitched through with quilting stitches. The term coverlet defines a bed cover of two layers (top and back) which are not quilted together. The distinction is, however, blurred by quilts from Cumbria, Ireland and the Isle of Man which are quilted but usually have no filling.

Chapter 1

1. Quoted in Averil Colby, *Quilting* (London: Batsford, 1972) p. 120.
2. Dorothy Osler, *Traditional British Quilts* (London: Batsford, 1987) p. 91.
3. Julia de Lacy Mann, "The Textile Industry: Machinery for Cotton, Flax, Wool, 1760-1850", in C. Singer, E. J. Holmyard, A. R. Hall and T. I. Williams (Eds), *A History of Technology*, vol. 4, *The Industrial Revolution c.1750-c.1850* (Oxford: Oxford University Press, 1957).
4. Edward Baines, *History of the Cotton Manufacture in Great Britain* (London: Fisher, Fisher & Jackson, 1835) p. 358.
5. Ibid.
6. Larch S. Garrad, "Quilting and Patchwork in the Isle of Man", in *Folklife*, 17 (1979), pp. 39-48.
7. Osler, p. 110.
8. Pers. comm., diary entries and information supplied by Dr Stafford Linsley, Department of Continuing Education, University of Newcastle, April 1998.
9. Ibid.
10. Dorothy Osler, "The Classic Strippy Quilt: Its Origins and Development", in *Quilt Studies*, 1 (1999), pp. 9-22.
11. Osler, *Traditional British Quilts*, p. 113.
12. *Newcastle Chronicle*, 14 January 1826, p. 2 (Newcastle City Library).
13. Newcastle City Library, undated.

Chapter 2

1. J. Lee, *Weardale Memories and Traditions* (published by the author, 1950) pp. 212-13.
2. Dorothy Osler, *Traditional British Quilts* (London: Batsford, 1987) p. 111.
3. A. Farnie, "The Textile Industry: Woven Fabrics", in C. Singer, E. J. Holmyard, A. R. Hall and T. I. Williams (Eds), *A History of Technology*, vol. 5, *The Late Nineteenth Century c.1850-c.1900* (Oxford: Oxford University Press, 1957).
4. Advertisement for Wheeler and Wilson's Sewing Machines by Messrs. Allen & Sons, Pant, Alnwick, in *The Alnwick Journal and Domestic Miscellany*, June 1870.
5. Advertisement for fabrics by James Allen & Son, General Drapers, in *The Alnwick Journal and Domestic Miscellany*, 15 July 1859.
6. For a full description of the quilt 'clubs' of North East England, see Osler, pp. 123-25.
7. Mavis FitzRandolph, *Traditional Quilting* (London: Batsford, 1954).
8. Ibid., p. 46
9. Osler, pp. 124-125.
10. See Dorothy Osler, "The Quilt Designers of North East England", in *Uncoverings 1998*, vol. 19 (1998), pp. 37-69, for a full account of this trade.
11. Ibid., p. 43.
12. FitzRandolph, p. 40-41.

Chapter 3

1. Dorothy Osler, *Traditional British Quilts* (London: Batsford, 1987) p. 125.
2. Mavis FitzRandolph, *Traditional Quilting* (London: Batsford, 1954) pp. 46-47.
3. Ibid., p. 47.
4. Ibid., p. 131.
5. Ibid.
6. Pers. comm., Mrs Wright, Allenheads, September 1995.
7. FitzRandolph, chapter 3.
8. Ibid., p. 50.
9. *Rural Industries*, Summer, 1932, p. 16.
10. S. Goodenough, *Jam and Jerusalem* (Glasgow/London: William Collins, 1977) quoted in Susan Marks, "Changing Perceptions of the Quilt in Twentieth Century Britain: A Personal Polemic", in *Quilt Studies* 2 (2000, forthcoming).
11. FitzRandolph, p. 50.

Chapter 4

1. Joan Finlinson, *Durham Quilting* (Durham: Durham Federation of Women's Institutes, n.d).
2. Letter to Lucy Krause, Craft Researcher, Shipley Art Gallery, Gateshead (Tyne & Wear Museums Craft Records, 5 June 1978).
3. Mavis FitzRandolph, *Traditional Quilting* (London: Batsford, 1954).
4. M. FitzRandolph and F. M. Fletcher, *Quilting* (Leicester, Dryad Press, 4th edition 1972).

Chapter 5

1. Amy Emms MBE, *Amy Emms Story of Durham Quilting* (Tunbridge Wells: Search Press, 1990).

Further Reading

Allan, Rosemary. *Quilts and Coverlets from Beamish Museum*. Stanley, Co. Durham: Beamish North of England Open Air Museum, 1987.

Colby, Averil. *Patchwork*. London: Batsford, 1958.

Colby, Averil. *Quilting*. London: Batsford, 1972.

Emms, Amy, MBE. *Amy Emms' Story of Durham Quilting*. Tunbridge Wells: Search Press, 1990.

FitzRandolph, Mavis. *Traditional Quilting*. London: Batsford, 1954.

FitzRandolph, Mavis & Fletcher, Florence. *Quilting*. Leicester, Dryad Press, 1972.

Hake, Elizabeth. *English Quilting Old and New*. London: Batsford, 1937.

Harris, Jennifer (Ed). *Take 4: New Perspectives on the British Art Quilt*. Manchester: Whitworth Art Gallery, 1998.

Osler, Dorothy. *Traditional British Quilts*. London: Batsford, 1987.

Osler, Dorothy. The quilt designers of North East England, *Uncoverings*, vol. 19 (1998), pp. 37-69 (Lincoln, NE: American Quilt Study Group).

Osler, Dorothy. The classic Strippy quilt: its origins and development, *Quilt Studies*, vol. 1 (1999), pp. 9-22 (Halifax: British Quilt Study Group).

Quilt Treasures: The Quilters' Guild Heritage Search. London: Deirdre McDonald Books, 1995.

Rae, Janet. *The Quilts of the British Isles*. London: Constable, New York: E. P. Dutton, 1987.

Ward, Anne. Quilting in the North of England, *Folk Life*, vol. 4 (1966), pp. 75-83.